London's Own Railway

THE
NORTH LONDON LINE
1846-2001

By
Dennis Lovett

Copyright IRWELL PRESS Ltd.,
ISBN 1-903266-12-2

First published in the United Kingdom in 2001
by Irwell Press Ltd.,
59A, High Street, Clophill,
Bedfordshire MK45 4BE
Printed by The Amadeus Press

The Author

The grandson of a signalman and the son of a train driver, Dennis Lovett is a third generation railwayman from Bletchley, Bucks. He joined the railway on leaving school before embarking on a career in journalism and publishing. He rejoined the railway eight years later where he was to hold a variety of posts within the Public Affairs organisations of the Southern Region, British Railways Board, Network South East, InterCity and North London Railways. He joined the North London Lines Modernisation Project as Communications Manager, on secondment from InterCity in October 1993. When the project passed to Railtrack in 1995 Dennis joined the train operating company responsible for operating the North London Line. He has since joined the public affairs team of Virgin Trains.

Married with two sons, the author still lives in his home town. An active railway modeller, he joined the Milton Keynes Model Railway Society on its formation in 1969. He served in a number of roles before being appointed Chairman in January 1988, a position he currently holds. Dennis has a keen interest in local history and more recently has been accepted into the membership of the North London Railway Historical Society.

Acknowledgements

Various authors have told me that this would be the most difficult of all pages to write and they are absolutely right! Such a complex project involved meeting and talking with many people, which has created an in-built fear of missing someone out. I am of course grateful to my many former colleagues who helped me initially to understand the complexities of this piece of railway and for their enthusiastic support, as I unravelled it further.

I am particularly indebted to those who supplied me with material and my special thanks go to former Public Affairs colleague Gary Smith. As the Southern Region's former Information Officer, Gary has a wealth of railway knowledge and his painstaking search through 30 or more years of railway periodicals has brought forth little-known facts and confirmed key dates and events for this book. Many others checked my manuscript, confirmed facts or pointed out silly errors, which hopefully have now all been corrected. These include: Chris Austin (formerly British Railways Board Public Affairs), Driver Ron Craddock (retired), Driver Percy Drummond (Watford), Gordon Eckersley, Chris Green (Chief Executive, Virgin Trains), David Hibbert, Peter Jarvis, Colin Judge, Signalman George Peacock (retired), Dick Riley, Driver Sid Rowson (retired), Don Smith (Train Crew Supervisor Watford and formerly of Broad Street), Mike Vincent (formerly InterCity) and Les Wood.

The North London Railway Historical Society has been a tremendous support and have provided me with information from a number of individuals and from their own records and publications. These include Peter Bishop, Jim Connor, Peter Lindop and David Hanson, Secretary of the Society.

Thanks also go to the staff of Bletchley Library, The Imperial War Museum, London Transport Museum Photographic Library, The National Railway Museum (York), The British Library Newspaper Library (Colindale, North London) and The Public Records Office (Kew). Thanks are also due to Doug Johnson, Stadium Manager at Chelsea Football Club, for confirming information relating to the club. Thanks are also due to Don Rowan (Archivist) and Derek Cookson (Librarian) at Tate & Lyle (Plaistow) for supplying historical information relating to their Silvertown plant.

Michael Minter Taylor, a railway author and close neighbour, kindly volunteered to check my manuscript for grammatical and other errors. His valuable contribution allowed me time to pursue the missing information, without having to worry about the mistakes made previously.

I am also grateful to the many photographers and photo libraries who allowed me access to their collections to illustrate this book. These include the former Central Photographic Unit of The British Railways Board (Waterloo), Network SouthEast (Euston), Richard Casserley (H.C. Casserley Collection), Percy Drummond, John Goss, Colin Marsden, Milepost 92.5 (Rev. Arthur Mace Collection), Brian Morrison, Gavin Morrison and R.C. Riley. Thanks are also due to Jim Connor for the original route maps and diagrams, produced from my very poor first efforts.

Finally to my wife Jenny and sons, Darren and Simon, for allowing this book to intrude into our home and for the occasional disruption it caused.
Dennis Lovett
May 2001

Cover photographs: *Top.* Train of empty wagons near Blackwall Junction on 23 August 1957. R.C.Riley, The Transport Treasury. *Bottom.* South Acton engine shed - see also page 14. National Railway Museum.

Contents

The North London is now seen as London's cross-city passenger link and that is a very important role, but we must not lose sight of its origins, to connect the London docks with the great new trunk route of Britain, the London & Birmingham Railway. Down at the docks, a vast infrastructure devoted to goods and material handling grew up. Photograph The National Railway Museum.

Preface

By David Hanson, Secretary, North London Railway Historical Society

The lumbering Park 0-6-0Ts were on freight and shunting throughout LMS days on the North London, though a number wandered away for specialist shunting far off on the system. Their famously last reprise was on the Cromford and High Peak line.

Little has been published over the years concerning the history of this complex urban line. Chisholm's booklet of 1902 contains useful contemporary material, but its historic side has some inaccuracies. Michael Robbins's masterly history, first published in 1937 had, of course, to be written without benefit of the company's own records. This small railway, with its multitude of connections and relationships, is extremely difficult to research; its minute books, now available at the Public Record Office, often tell a different story to its shareholders' reports, and imply a great deal of politics and intrigue. The truth is frequently difficult to establish, and can only be interpreted after consulting the records of other companies.

It is the aim of the North London Railway Historical Society to carry out such research and to publish the results. Various members have examined Dennis's manuscript to the best of their current knowledge, and research continues into this most unusual railway. The Society is grateful to Dennis for his kind donation of the royalties from this book, which will be used to further this work.

Post-war reconstruction – Primrose Hill in 1965. The work amounted in most cases to little more than a cheap frontage and a decade or more later many of the stations looked as shabby as ever. Be prepared for grim and grimy stations in this book!

The seat(s) of power – the NLR Board Room. Photograph The National Railway Museum.

Introduction

'Before you can establish where you are going – it is necessary to know where you have come from'

In October 1993 I was seconded by InterCity to work part time on the North London Line Modernisation Project as Communications Manager, joining the project team on a full-time basis when InterCity head-quarters closed in March 1994. I suddenly found myself working on a piece of railway about which I knew very little and soon discovered that this was a line with a very complex history indeed. I have found throughout my railway public affairs career that it was important to read up on lines such as this, in order to have the answers, so that when journalists and others asked the questions, I either knew the answer or where to find it in the quickest possible time!

I would often attend meetings or brief journalists about the project, when questions would inevitably be asked about the line's past. The modernisation of the North London Line created a great deal of attention and in order to understand its future, it was necessary to get to grips with the past. When did this station open? why was it renamed? or when did this junction open? Over the two years I worked on the project, such information was collated. It was not then the intention to produce a book but as the project passed to others, I was persuaded that the collected information should be placed before a wider audience. Little I did I realise that when my day to day involvement with the project finished, that it would take so long to achieve the desired result.

Such research is beyond the abilities of any one person and I am, therefore, grateful to the many colleagues and friends who assisted me during the five years that this project has taken. Fortunately, I was introduced to the North London Railway Historical Society who have made material available, assisted me when the going became difficult and more importantly, painstakingly checked the contents during the various stages to publication. The enthusiasm and support from many for this line has enabled completion of what I trust, will be a useful source for both historians and for those involved in the future shaping of public transport in North London.

The royalties from this publication have been donated to the North London Railway Historical Society, so that they can continue their research and produce further publication in the years ahead. I wish them every success in their endeavours.

Dennis Lovett
Bletchley, Milton Keynes
May 2001

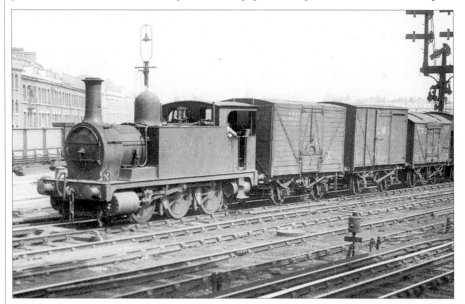

Above. Ancient postcard print showing a North London train of the usual impossible length at Haringay, on the Great Northern – see Chapter Seven.

The original frontage to Broad Street Station, 3 February 1868.

Every company had a finger in the East London pie... Photograph National Railway Museum.

Chapter One
Opening up London

The arrival of railways in the capital

Before the building of the railways from the 1830s, the principle form of transport for commodities destined for an expanding London was by water (sea, canal or river). Roads were slow and tortuous; only the wealthy could travel the turnpikes on the stage-coach system which served different parts of the country. London itself was a tightly packed community much smaller than the Greater London known today; almost all of the area now served by the North London Line consisted in the 1830s of small villages amid green fields.

Although it may appear at first irrelevant to the building of what was to become the North London Railway (NLR), it was the first line north of the River Thames that was to become the lynch pin around which the NLR system would develop. It is therefore necessary to look at this scheme in detail before tackling the forerunner of the NLR itself. It is also important to bear in mind that the London & North Western company, as successors to the London & Birmingham Railway, would play an important role in North London development as partner, adviser and financier.

The London & Birmingham Railway

The proposal to build a railway between London and Birmingham was spurred on by the success of early schemes in other parts of the country. The area now known as Euston was chosen for the London terminus as early as 1831, though it was to be a further six years before it saw any trains. At that time London was expanding to the limits of the 'new' road, now known as Euston Road, the M25 of its day. Much of the land in the Euston area was owned by the Duke of Grafton whose ancestral seat, Euston Hall near Thetford in Norfolk, gave its name to Euston Square and other nearby streets.

The land around Euston at that time was mainly used for dairy farming or market gardening. Farming interests ensured that when the London & Birmingham Railway Act reached the House of Lords in June 1832, it was rejected, despite having been accepted by the House of Commons four months earlier.

The promoters of the London & Birmingham submitted the Act again in the following year and this time they were successful, for it received the Royal Assent on 6th May 1833. The only amendment was that the terminus would be Chalk Farm and not Euston. The conflict with the landowners was resolved in the twelve months between the Parliamentary Bills simply by the railway increasing its compensation considerably, and the same policy was adopted in 1835, so that the line could be extended to its original planned terminus on Euston Road.

Euston station opened to the public on 20th July 1837, with trains initially running to Boxmoor, now Hemel Hempstead. The official opening took place on 17th September 1838, when trains began running between England's two largest cities, London and Birmingham.

Joining up with the London & Birmingham

With the first section of railway in north London sanctioned, it was not long before others were casting envious eyes in that direction. In 1836 came an Act of Parliament authorising the London Grand Junction Railway to build from Skinner Street, in the City of London (near Holborn Viaduct—opened 2nd March 1874—was later to be built) to connect with the London & Birmingham near Camden Town, 3 miles 4 furlongs away. The line was to be carried on brick arches. However, the project never progressed beyond the planning stages.

In 1845, three companies proposed to construct lines, from what is now

A typical freight rumbles through Hackney behind one of the NLR 0-6-0Ts, carrying the characteristic 'target' number. This would be in LMS days. Coastal coal had come through Poplar Dock, to be carried into the great metropolitan hinterland by the NLR, since the 1850s.

Old Ford, a postcard view.

'Docklands', to connect with the London & Birmingham Railway. One of the three bodies held a meeting on the 30th October 1845 at the offices of Timothy Tyrrell, 5 Church Passage, Guildhall, with a view to forming a Board of Directors to take the plans forward. Present were: Alexander Beattie, Edward Maxwell Daniel, Henry Davidson, Pascoe St. Leger Grenfell, John Alexander Hankey, Thomas Seddon Kelsall, John Lambert, Charles Lyall, William Henri [sic] Thomas, Thomas Young who together with Rt .Hon. George Anson M.P., George Reid, T.S. Richards, John Scott and James Seager formed the provisional Board of Directors of the company, to be called 'The East & West India Docks & Birmingham

Homerton station. From early on, the NLR stations were not really like others; in some cases they had to be 'slotted' into the street pattern and even where they were built in open country, the town soon washed up around them. The company competed for sign space in the crowded London streetscapes and proclaimed itself wherever possible. The vaults of Homerton station frontage are surmounted by a plain pediment – NORTH LONDON RAILWAY HOMERTON STATION and the bridge reminds the (then rather well-to-do) locals that it carries the NORTH LONDON RAILWAY. The Great Northern gets in on the act a little cheekily, insinuating a detailed sign for its own Hackney Wick 'Goods, Coal and Potato Depôt' nearby. The last two, of course, were absolute essentials of Edwardian urban life...

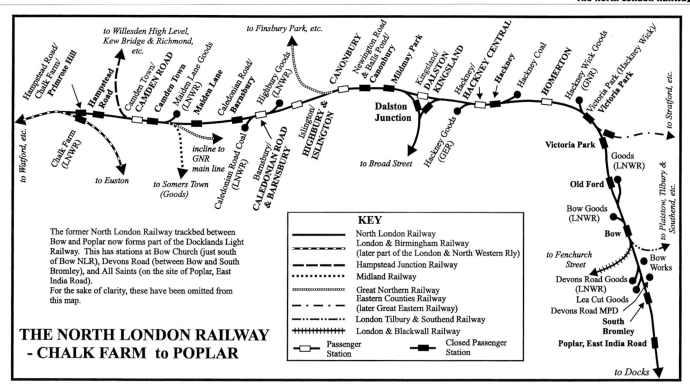

The former North London Railway trackbed between Bow and Poplar now forms part of the Docklands Light Railway. This has stations at Bow Church (just south of Bow NLR), Devons Road (between Bow and South Bromley), and All Saints (on the site of Poplar, East India Road).
For the sake of clarity, these have been omitted from this map.

THE NORTH LONDON RAILWAY - CHALK FARM to POPLAR

KEY

——————	North London Railway
– – – –	London & Birmingham Railway (later part of the London & North Western Rly)
· · · · · ·	Hampstead Junction Railway
··········	Midland Railway
▪▪▪▪▪▪▪▪	Great Northern Railway
– · – · –	Eastern Counties Railway (later Great Eastern Railway)
– ·· – ··	London Tilbury & Southend Railway
++++++++	London & Blackwall Railway
☐ Passenger Station	■ Closed Passenger Station

Junction Railway'. The East & West India Docks & Birmingham Junction Railway Act duly received the Royal Assent on 20th August 1846, to construct a line 8 miles in length. It was left to the ponderously titled E&WID&BJR to promote and build the line from the London & Birmingham to the docks at Blackwall.

In the same year, on 16th July 1846, the London & Birmingham Railway amalgamated with two other railways from the North and Midlands (the Grand Junction Railway and the Manchester & Birmingham Railway) to form a new company, the London & North Western Railway (LNWR). It was with this company that the East & West India Docks & Birmingham Junction Railway would form a junction some years later.

It would appear that the E&WID&BJR had the support of the newly formed LNWR from the start. The LNWR was no doubt attracted by what the docks might contribute to its goods figures, and so it put up a great deal of the share capital. In 1846, the issue consisted of 12,000 shares of which 8,000 were owned by LNWR and 4,000 available to the public; of these 1,000 were acquired by the West India Dock Company. The issue allowed for a minimum of six Directors and a maximum of thirteen. The E&WID&BJR headquarters was accommodated in the same offices as the LNWR, at Euston.

The building of the E&WID&BJR was not without its problems. Due to difficulties in raising funds, construction was slow and the first section of line from Islington to Bow Junction (where it formed a junction with the London & Blackwall Railway) did not open until 26th September 1850.

Some sources say the line was built purely to carry goods traffic but this cannot have been the case, for passenger stations were provided from the start, at Bow, Hackney and Islington. The E&WID&BJR Board Minutes of the 20th February 1849 reported that *works have been so arranged that all sections of the line referred to in the passenger timetable will be completed simultaneously with the portion through Camden Town*.

Following opening, *Herapath's Journal* (19th October 1850), gives a journey

Much of the NLR and its stations came to be bywords for decay and decrepitude. This is the less than appetising interior of Canonbury station in the winter of 1965.

Top. Even a daily pinta (the year is 1965) would not go far to relieving this dreary prospect upon leaving Canonbury station! The sign at the end reads: FOR TRAINS TO WILLESDEN JUNCTION RICHMOND & WATFORD. It demonstrates the strategic usefulness of the NLR, but the picture illustrates the neglect of this wonderful London asset.

Middle. Canonbury again, November 1965. It was not a prospect to encourage patrons!

Bottom. The great bulk of Canonbury station looks doomed in the swinging sixties.

time of 25 minutes from Fenchurch Street to Islington, including a Stepney stop on the London & Blackwall line. Trains were reported as leaving Fenchurch Street at 15 minute intervals. The same article records that the Directors had reached agreement with the LNWR for the supply of locomotives to work the first services. The edition dated 7th December 1850 reports that the line was currently passenger only and that the introduction of goods traffic was dependant on the opening of the junction with the LNWR.

Linking up with 'the other' L&B

The first passenger trains to operate over what was to become the North London Railway (NLR) were operated in conjunction with the first line to serve the East End of London—the London & Blackwall.

The London & Blackwall had opened on 4th July 1840, as a 5ft. gauge rope worked line. Its beginnings, however, could be traced back to the 1820s, when promoters were anxious to connect passengers from the Blackwall Docks with the City of London. Boat traffic was considerable and congestion not uncommon, with craft pressing to sail into the City. This led to development in the East End and Blackwall benefited accordingly, becoming the principal passenger ship terminus for London.

The London & Blackwall was soon promoting an extension to join up with the Eastern Counties Railway (ECR) near Bow, thus gaining access to Stratford. The ECR was not, however, an enthusiastic partner in the London & Blackwall's objectives. The London & Blackwall extension was required to terminate at Victoria Park & Bow, where the ECR also constructed platforms on its main line from Bishopsgate, and some LBR services were forced to terminate short at Bow & Bromley. With relationships at an all-time low, it took a petition to Parliament to sort out the arguments, though eventually the two companies worked together in harmony.

During the disputes with the ECR, the London & Blackwall Directors were actively monitoring the approaching E&WID&BJR, and soon formed a working partnership. The service was shown in timetables as subsidiary to The London & Blackwall Railway, which of course, it never was. As a result, mileages were worked out from Fenchurch Street and trains travelling towards Fenchurch Street were designated Up and those to

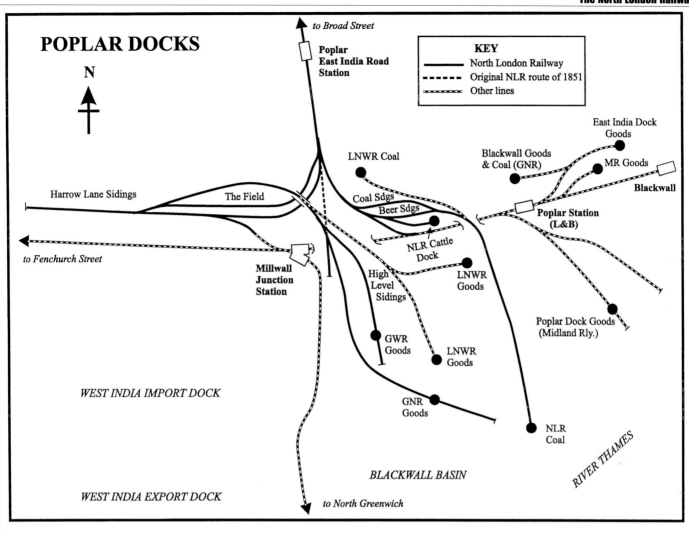

POPLAR DOCKS

N

to Broad Street

Poplar
East India Road
Station

KEY

North London Railway
Original NLR route of 1851
Other lines

East India Dock
Goods

LNWR Coal

Blackwall Goods
& Coal (GNR)

MR Goods

Harrow Lane Sidings

The Field

Coal Sdgs

Beer Sdgs

Blackwall

Poplar Station
(L&B)

to Fenchurch Street

Millwall
Junction
Station

NLR Cattle
Dock

LNWR
Goods

High
Level
Sidings

Poplar Dock Goods
(Midland Rly.)

GWR
Goods

LNWR
Goods

WEST INDIA IMPORT DOCK

GNR
Goods

NLR
Coal

RIVER THAMES

WEST INDIA EXPORT DOCK

BLACKWALL BASIN

to North Greenwich

Islington Down. In later years, following the opening of the Broad Street Line (see Chapter 4), Poplar became the Up destination and Richmond the Down.

The link with the LNWR
The section from Islington to the London & Birmingham main line suffered from engineering difficulties, caused mainly by London Clay and the collapse of seven arches near Maiden Lane, which carried the line over the Great Northern Railway's (GNR) main line, being built at the same time. The section from Islington to Camden Town opened on 7th December 1850. The line was not fully completed until 15th February 1851, when it formed a junction at Chalk Farm (later known at Primrose Hill) with the now renamed London & Birmingham, the LNWR. Passenger trains terminated at a temporary station called Hampstead Road, short of the junction itself, the official boundary between the NLR and LNWR systems. The section beyond Camden Road had been delayed by the need to acquire some dwellings on the route, which caused the work to be temporarily abandoned, until negotiations had been concluded.

Defying the creeping dereliction so evident elsewhere on the NLR (at least out on the platform in this view) Camden Road retains much of its stolid, respectable style in June 1955.

Top. Down below it was a question of faded glory – a glorious wood panelled interior marred by later accretions.

Middle. Very often it was the streets round about that were run down and awaiting that blight of the 1960s, 'comprehensive redevelopment'. Many NLR stations were caught up in this, and were accordingly as dilapidated as their surroundings. This was typical – around the corner from Camden Road station in 1955, however gentrified the streets may be now, they were then insalubrious in the extreme.

Bottom. Another soot-caked pile, Camden Road station in June 1955.

Following completion of work, at a cost of some £800,000 (1850 prices), the line became an instant success, 97,000 passengers being carried during the first month of operation!

Arrival at the docks
1st January 1852 saw the opening of the line south from Bow to Poplar and the West India Docks for freight traffic only. At Poplar, the NLR owned 28 acres of docks and goods depots. Three large goods yards were eventually established at Poplar – Harrow Lane, The Field and High Level, providing some 14 miles of sidings. Access to West India an Millwall Docks was obtained via Millwall Junction. Vast amounts of traffic were carried; at its peak, for instance, 700 wagons a week were exchanged between Harrow Lane yard and Millwall Junction. Passenger trains did not reach Poplar until the introduction of a service from Broad Street in 1866 (see Chapter 4).

Blackwall Docks
Blackwall Docks had two sites, Blackwall and Canning Town, both on Bow Creek at the mouth of the River Lea. Blackwall was used extensively for grain, and five barges could be loaded simultaneously.

Millwall Docks
The main docks were centred on Poplar. Dock basins included: Poplar, East India (with both import and export docks), West India (import and export docks) and South, served by the NLR, Great Eastern (formerly ECR), Great Northern, Great Western, Midland and LNWR, all with their own extensive warehouses and sidings. NLR trains got to the docks by reversing at Harrow Lane sidings to reach Millwall Junction, south of Poplar station.

The NLR
When the E&WID&BJR became the NLR on 1st January 1853, there were twelve Directors, six of whom came from the LNWR. Those with dual portfolios included the Deputy Chairman of the NLR, Richard Creed, who was also an LNWR Director and the LNWR's Chairman, Major General George Anson MP, who was a Director of the NLR. Company Secretary was Harry Chubb who, while answerable to the Board, was not a member of it.

Top. **They were different times indeed on the Camden Road (the station building is to the left) in 1955, though the vast girders of the NLR dominate the scene still. The trolleybus wires have long gone of course and the cigarette adverts are a lot more subtle; salt seems to have lost its charm and Coca Cola at least had an attractive bottle. A tired poster at the extreme left reads VOTE NICHOLSON X COMMUNIST.**

Above. **Camden Road in June 1955, with A. Brilliant's traditional 'fag shop'. Note the age-blackened but once noble title high above. You would wait long today to catch the road clear of traffic like this...**

London in the 1850s devoured coal, most of it coming from the North East to the docks by coastal shipping. The NLR, in what can only be described (retrospectively) as a bad move, allowed The Northumberland & Durham Coal Company to move its own coal over the route, using its own rolling stock, for which the NLR received an annual sum of £10,000. This method of operation led to conflict and the NLR was forced in 1859 to rectify the situation by buying out the coal company's interest and rolling stock, for £43,000.

Passenger services continued much as they had before. The potential of this cross-London route was by now attracting the attention of other companies, keen to link up with it. The coat of arms of the original E&WID&BJR lived on, passing to the NLR in 1853. It incorporated four heraldic devices represented clockwise from top left, East India Dock Company, City of Birmingham, West India Dock Company, City of London.

Connecting Lines
1: The North London Incline
An incline linking the NLR with the Great Northern main line was opened in 1853, joining the NLR at St. Pancras Junction (not to be confused with St. Pancras station, which was not to open until 1868). This line was known as North London Incline, and construction was only got underway after the GNR took legal advice. Provision for this short connecting line was made in the original E&WID&BJR 1846 Act of Parliament, to enable the GNR line, being built at the same time, access to the docks. There was a reluctance for the E&WID&BJR to undertake this work, but Vice Chancellor Parker ruled, on 23rd July 1852, that they must provide the GNR with the connections originally envisaged. The GNR, however, which owned the land, decided to leave nothing to chance and apart from the laying of the actual junction undertook all the construction itself. This work was completed in June 1853.

The 29 chain North London Incline was improved between 1859 and 1862. The original gradient was quite steep and measures were taken to reduce it and give a more gradual approach, the Midland contributing to the cost of the work. The MR deposited plans for a goods yard and shed in February 1860 and again for the building of the London Extension (Bedford-St. Pancras) in 1864. The widening of the NLR viaduct over the GNR main line took place at the same time.

While serving primarily for freight traffic, the North London Incline was used by the Royal Train, conveying Queen Victoria from Gosport (nearest station at that time on the mainland to Osborne House on the Isle of Wight) to Balmoral. The incline was used again during 1860 and 1868 when the Queen journeyed from Balmoral to Windsor.

2: Victoria Park - Stratford
In 1854, the Eastern Counties Railway opened its line from Victoria Park (Hackney Wick) to Channelsea Junction near Stratford, for goods traffic on 15th Au-

Everyone was there – the GWR goods 'depôt' at Poplar again.

gust and to passengers from 16th October, although no station was provided at the junction at Victoria Park until 1st July 1856. In 1862, the ECR became a major constituent of the newly formed Great Eastern Railway and in 1866 a new station (resited to the north west of the previous structure) was provided at Victoria Park, to serve both GER and NLR trains. Full details of this line can be found in Chapter 6.

3: Bow - Poplar - Blackwall
The section from Bow to Poplar (East India Road) opened for passenger traffic on 1st August 1866, with through trains running from Broad Street. This service was extended to Blackwall in 1870, via (though not stopping there) Poplar GE,

adjacent to Brunswick Wharf. This was an important passenger ferry terminal at the time, with regular services to Gravesend, Southend and Margate. In July 1890, the passenger service from Poplar (East India Road) to Blackwall was withdrawn and the junction removed.

4: Bow - Bromley
On 18th May 1869 the North London Railway opened a spur from Bow to Bromley Junction on the London, Tilbury & Southend Railway (LT&SR), with a shuttle service introduced from Bow to Plaistow. It was also used for excursion traffic, mainly to the popular resort of Southend. Commencing in the summer of 1869, until 1881, trains were run from Chalk Farm to Thames Haven on the

LT&S, to connect with steamers for Margate.

5: Canonbury - Finsbury Park (GNR)
In 1871 the GNR announced plans for the construction of a line, 1 mile 31 chains long, from Finsbury Park to Canonbury, including the 544 yard Canonbury Tunnel. The Act of Parliament for the widening of the GNR main line and associated schemes received the Royal Assent on 18th July 1872. The building of this line also required a major reconstruction of the GNR's Finsbury Park station, the line opening for freight on 14th December 1874 and passengers on 18th January 1875. GNR proposals to operate passenger trains over this line were rejected by the LNWR but a compromise deal resulted in the NLR operating services to GNR destinations (see Chapter 7).

6: NLR - Churchyard Sidings (known as the North London Incline)
A further spur was opened on 1st November 1887 from the NLR to Churchyard Sidings, the MR goods establishment north of St. Pancras station. Its purpose was the transfer of goods vehicles, notably cattle wagons bound for the Metropolitan Cattle Market at Caledonian Road or the nearby slaughterhouse. This was located on a brick and metal viaduct, a single line which ran alongside the MR goods shed, before crossing the throat and reaching the NLR. All the sidings were owned by the MR.

Station openings and renamings (see also Appendix 1)
When services began from the London & Blackwall Railway's Fenchurch Street terminus on 26th September 1850, the

The section from Bow to Poplar (East India Road) opened for passengers in August 1866, with through trains running from Broad Street, and was extended to Blackwall in 1870. Twenty years later, in July 1890, the passenger service from East India Road to Blackwall was withdrawn and the junction removed. It was a place unimaginable now, proud and magnificent at the heart of empire, as this picture shows, with its noble buildings and masted ships. Much of this quality was lost as the economy, commerce and prosperity of the district altered. The sign reads *TO THE EAST INDIA ROAD STATION* (pointing to the right) *Trains every 15 minutes to BROAD STREET, DALSTON, CAMDEN TOWN (WILLESDEN JUNCTION) FOR LONDON AND NORTH WESTERN Co's TRAINS*. The whole dock installation, with the curious cranes, looks new.

Everyday work at Poplar Docks in the Nineteenth Century. A seven plank wagon (greatly extended in capacity – like its neighbour) is posed up on the iron platform, raised by hydraulic ram. This whole lot may look primitive but it represented a materials handling revolution that underpinned industrial Britain.

E&WID&BJR had three stations open for traffic, at Bow, Hackney and Islington. Stations soon followed at Kingsland, on 9th November 1850 and Camden Town, on 7th December.

The opening of the line to its junction with the LNWR resulted in the building of a temporary terminus at Hampstead Road on 9th June 1851, a more permanent structure being provided from 5th June 1855. Caledonian Road station followed on 10th June 1852, Newington Road & Balls Pond on 1st September 1858, Homerton on 1st October 1868, and Mildmay Park on 1st January 1880. Camden Town was renamed Camden Road in 1853. A new station was opened to the west, following reconstruction in conjunction with the quadrupling scheme, on 1st July 1870. The station reverted back to its 1850 name of Camden Town.

Hampstead Road was renamed Chalk Farm on 1st December 1862. In August 1869 the LNWR Engineer at Stafford prepared a drawing for the new station at Chalk Farm. The contract was awarded in April 1870 and the station entrance opened on 2nd October 1871. Work was complete on 24th May 1872. The station currently remains in situ (2001) although disused and the former station booking office is used as a retail

Pouring rain and a cracked image do little to relieve the thoroughly faded glory of Highbury and Islington station, March 1952.

Inside Highbury and Islington, 20 October 1950. The NLR was never short of space...

outlet. In recent times this station was known as Primrose Hill.

Islington station became Islington & Highbury on 1st June 1864, but was altered to Highbury & Islington on 1st July 1872, following rebuilding as part of the quadrupling work. Old Ford, between Victoria Park and Bow, opened on 1st July 1867.

On 1st July 1870 Caledonian Road station was renamed Barnsbury, while Newington Road & Balls Pond became Canonbury. Maiden Lane opened on 1st July 1887, although a goods depot had been established by the NLR as early as

June 1867. The goods depot was transferred to the LNWR in 1871.

A footbridge from Hackney station to the nearby Hackney Downs station of the GER was opened on 1st December 1885. The GER relocated its Bow Road station on 4th April 1892, when GER trains ceased calling at the NLR's Bow station. A covered footway was provided between the two.

Quadrupling

Before quadrupling of the line (authorised by Act of Parliament in 1861) could be undertaken, rebuilding work was necessary on several stations. A new Canonbury station, to the west of the original, opened on 1st December 1870 and the new Barnsbury, to the east of the previous station, opened on 21st November 1870. Hackney, resited to the west of the previous station, opened on 1st December that year. The opening of the rebuilt station saw 'Islington & Highbury' transposed to 'Highbury & Islington' on 1st July 1872, as already stated. These stations were constructed in the NLR 'house style' of architecture. Bow was also rebuilt at this time, although the work was not undertaken as part of the quad-

Another fine exterior – parking would never be like this again!

Contretemps at Bow – a much repaired but still dramatic NRM image. This is the crash referred to in the text in this Chapter, concerning the errant No.46. National Railway Museum.

rupling scheme. The stations were designed by E. H. Horne, while the building work was undertaken at most stations by Wicks, Bangs & Co. of Bow.

With station work well underway or completed, work commenced on quadrupling the line itself, from Dalston Western Junction to Camden Road. The work was undertaken between 1870 and 1873, the original tracks becoming the 'No.2 lines' and the new formation the No.1 lines. Each pair of tracks had their own signal boxes.

Murders
1: Thomas Briggs
On 9th July 1864 the NLR had the unfortunate distinction of dealing with the first ever murder to take place on a train. Thomas Briggs, a senior bank clerk who lived at Hackney, caught the 9.45pm train from Fenchurch Street to Chalk Farm. When the train called at Hackney, two passengers bound for Islington & Highbury found a blood stained seat and items belonging to Mr Briggs. The Guard was alerted and the vehicle removed to Bow for investigation. Whilst this was taking place, the crew of a southbound Up train noticed something on the track and stopped to examine it. They discovered Mr Briggs, who was still alive, and took him to an adjacent public house, *The Mitford Castle*, so that a Doctor could attend to him. Unfortunately he died the following day.

It later turned out that Briggs had been attacked in his compartment, robbed of various items including his watch and snuff box, and was then thrown from the train. The murder generated a great deal of newspaper coverage and rewards of £100 for information were offered by both the Government and the NLR. As a result, a jeweller who had brought some items from a 'foreign' gentleman came forward. The person selling had also bought an item from the jeweller during the negotiations and had given it to a young lady as a present. The father of the lady then stepped forward and

identified the gentleman as Franz Muller, a German tailor. Muller had already left his lodgings bound for New York, aboard a ship from London docks. Despite the delay of several days, two Police officers were sent to Liverpool to join a faster ship, which duly arrived in New York before the one from London. They were able to arrest Muller and escorted him back to Liverpool. Following trial in London, Muller was sentenced to death and hanged outside Newgate Prison in one of London's last public executions, on 14th November 1864.

Following these tragic events, the NLR cut holes in the partitions between compartments and for many years these were nicknamed 'Muller' or 'Muller's Lights'. *The Mitford Castle* is today known as the *Top O' The Morning* and still contains several cuttings and photographs of the murder.

2: Manfred Masset
On 9th January 1900, at 9 am, Louise Masset became the first woman to be hanged in the new century. She had been convicted of murdering her 3½ year old son, Manfred, and dumping his body in the ladies lavatory on Platform 3 at Dalston Junction on 27th October 1899.

Masset was arrested and charged on 31st October, four days after the murder took place. Louise protested her innocence, claiming she had put the boy into the care of two ladies in Brighton. An initial hearing took place on 4th November before the North London Police Court and lasted just three minutes. A week's remand was granted to allow the Police more time to track down the witnesses, who had reported the body in the lavatory. The trial commenced at the Old Bailey on 13th December and lasted five days. Masset was defended by Lord Coleridge, whilst Mr Matthews prosecuted for the Crown. The jury retired and took just 30 minutes to reach a guilty verdict.

Although Masset protested her innocence throughout her trial, on her way to

the gallows she confessed the crime and did not resist during the final preparations. *The East London Advertiser* of 13th January 1900 reported that a large crowd stood outside Newgate Prison waiting for the black flag to be hoisted. They gave a hearty cheer on its appearance and dispersed.

3: William Starchfield
On 9th January 1914 a five year old child, William Starchfield, was found dead underneath a seat on the 4.14pm from Chalk Farm. It was established that the boy had actually been a passenger on the 1.59pm train from the same station and had been strangled during the course of that journey, the train having subsequently made two further trips between Broad Street and Chalk Farm before discovery of the body. Following information received from a signalman, the boy's father was charged with his murder, but the prosecution case collapsed and he was acquitted. The father later worked as a newspaper seller at Liverpool Street station and was killed during an air raid on the station in 1941.

Accidents
A boiler explosion took place at Camden Road on 14th July 1855, involving the Stothert & Slaughter 2-4-0T No.10. At around 5.10pm, the boiler barrel exploded. leaving the fire tubes exposed. Fortunately the crew, who were brewing tea during the station stop, escaped serious injury. In his report, the Inspecting Officer, Lt.-Col Wynne, concluded that one of the iron plates was defective and had not been welded correctly during the locomotive's manufacture. The official report, however, gives the name of the station as Camden *Town*. It had been renamed Camden Road in 1853!

In 1869, No.46 was derailed, ending up at the bottom of the embankment between Victoria Park and Homerton. The engine was travelling light and received only minor damage. The crew were uninjured.

A serious incident occurred at Old Ford in January 1882, when a train bound for Poplar struck a derailed coal wagon. Five passengers were killed, the only occasion in which an NLR train was involved in a fatal crash.

Another accident occurred at Islington & Highbury on the 20th January 1869, concerning a Mr Bridges, who was a passenger on a train which was longer than the station platform. He alighted on arrival and fell underneath the train. Unfortunately, the train then pulled forward to allow the remaining coaches to be alongside the platform, killing Mr Bridges in the process. The matter was eventually settled in the House of Lords, with the NLR paying his widow considerable compensation.

Further Expansion
With the linking of the docks to the LNWR, the original objectives had been met. It was not long, however, before further plans would evolve. The rapid expansion of the NLR was about to begin.

Period gaucherie at the little engine shed at South Acton. This time (see also the cover picture) the engine is 4-4-0T No.29.

Chapter Two
Towards Surrey

The North & South Western Junction Railway (Old Oak Junction - Kew)

It was not long before railway promoters were looking to build lines into south west London and Surrey from the LNWR's London to Birmingham main line. A scheme for connecting the LNWR with the London & South Western Railway (LSWR) at Kew was first promoted in 1848 and rejected by Parliament; in 1851 it was resubmitted and authorised. The line was built from what is now Willesden Junction (there was no station there at that time) to join the LSWR's Hounslow loop line at Kew Junction. Trains began running to a specially constructed Kew platform in 1853, although a permanent station did not follow until a couple of years later. Although the LNWR and LSWR promoted the building of the line, they concentrated on goods traffic, allowing the passenger service to be operated by the NLR.

Originally a single track line, goods traffic began on 15th February 1853, while passenger trains began operating from Camden Road to Kew on 1st August 1853. Trains on this route used the LNWR main line for the short 3 miles 900 yards stretch between Hampstead

Road and what is now Willesden Junction. This would soon lead to congestion and the building of the Hampstead Junction Railway (see Chapter Three). The only intermediate station between Willesden Junction and Kew was a modest affair at Acton. The somewhat Spartan terminus at Kew, on the western side of the triangular junction, was replaced by a new station at Kew Bridge on the eastern side, on 1st February 1862. This gave cross-platform interchange with the LSWR. The original Kew station remained open for another four years to receive special trains. For a short period, trains continued beyond Kew. During the summer of 1854, the NLR introduced a service to Windsor, but this was not a success and was withdrawn five months later.

The LSWR lost interest in the route and finally disposed of its holding in 1871. Leading up to this, the NLR board meeting of 15 December 1870 heard that it was proceeding with the taking over of the lease of the N&SWJR, by establishing a Joint Committee with the LNWR and MR. At the meeting of the board held on 16 February 1871, details of the revised lease agreements had been re-

ceived. The meeting on the 16th March agreed to the terms of the N&SWJR lease, subject to final approval from the LNWR.

The Hammersmith Branch (North & South Western Junction Railway)

A branch from South Acton to Hammersmith opened for goods on 1st May 1857, and for passengers on 8th April 1858, amid great controversy. The building of the line was sanctioned by the Directors, but Shareholders forced an enquiry which was extremely critical, finding little justification for its construction in the first place.

Trains ran at first from Acton station and reversed at the junction (known initially as Acton Gate House and later Hammersmith Branch Junction) before continuing to the terminus a mile and 40 chains away. Because of the lack of a station at the junction, passenger traffic was worked by detaching and attaching vehicles there. Later, there was a form of 'slip coach' working, which survived until the opening of South Acton station, but this was a long way removed from the specially built 'slip coaches' employed by the Great Western and other companies. When the station at South Acton was opened in 1880, the branch was extended a short distance to meet it. The terminus was renamed Hammersmith & Chiswick in the same year.

Traffic levels never matched expectations even after 1909, when a steam rail motor was introduced as an economy measure and three additional halts were opened en-route, at Rugby Road, Woodstock Road and Bath Road. The branch closed for passenger traffic, as part of country-wide wartime economies, on 1st January 1917, although it was to remain open for freight until the mid-1960s (see Chapter 14). An engine shed was provided at the terminus in the early days and the N&SWJR's only locomotive was kept there until 1860.

Acton stations and depot

Acton station was rebuilt in 1876, while South Acton opened on 1st January 1880. The N&SWJR Board, at its meeting held on 15th October 1869, approved construction of a new engine shed and associated sidings at the junction of the Hammersmith Branch, for use by the NLR. A tender submitted by Mr Cardens for £1,100 to carry out the construction work was accepted. The new facilities were in use by early 1870, although a map published in 1873 did not reflect these changes. The shed closed in 1916 with the electrification of the Kew Bridge and Richmond services, so leaving Devons Road, Bow, the only remaining NLR running shed. The building at South Acton survived until 8th December 1954, when it was destroyed in a gale.

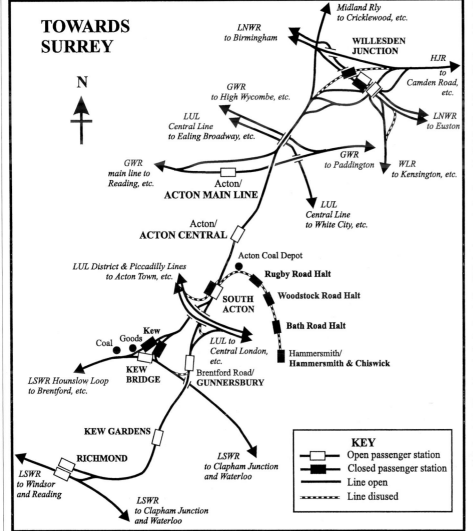

South Acton on the North & South Western Junction section, opened in 1880 was, by the 1960s, a fairly typical North London establishment, stripped of staff, neglected, dilapidated and plainly marked down for extinction.

London & South Western Railway (South Acton - Richmond)

Richmond, ten miles west of the centre of London, is an ancient town on the banks of the Thames. Local businesses and railway promoters were anxious to exploit the traffic of the town and as early as the 1830s there were several daily stagecoaches from Richmond to the City of London. Various railway proposals were fought over but it was not until the Richmond Railway Bill received the Royal Assent, on 21st July 1845, that any came to fruition. The first train left Nine Elms (Waterloo did not open until 1848) for Richmond on 27th July 1846, and was operated on behalf of the Richmond Railway Company by the LSWR, from the outset.

The arrival of the railway in Richmond was quickly justified and by now neighbouring towns such as Staines and Windsor were looking to be included in the rapidly expanding network. After several abortive attempts, the LSWR proposals were accepted and trains began running west of Richmond to Datchet (Berkshire) on 22nd August 1848.

By 1857, the LSWR was keen to see an extension of the N&SWJR from Kew to Richmond, but was unable to interest its LNWR partner. An independent scheme for a line from Kew to Richmond was rejected in 1857 by The House of Lords, so the LSWR began running services (on 20th May 1858) from Twickenham and Richmond to Hampstead Heath, Camden Road and Fenchurch Street, over NLR tracks by a somewhat complicated route. These trains had to reverse at both Barnes and Kew, resulting in an unnecessarily slow journey and in 1863, just to complicate matters further, trains were extended to Kingston-upon-Thames! The link between Acton Junction (now South Acton) and Richmond was eventually completed by the LSWR opening a line itself. Known as the Richmond Extension Line, it opened on 1st January 1869 and although owned by the LSWR, was used by other companies including the NLR. The line included intermediate stations at Brentford Road (now Gunnersbury) and Kew Gardens.

On the same day (1st January 1869) the LSWR opened the 3 mile 60 chain line from Brentford Road to Kensington (Addison Road), which was promoted as the Kensington & Richmond Railway. Intermediate stations were provided at Turnham Green, Shaftesbury Road, Hammersmith Grove Road and Shepherds Bush. Kensington (Addison Road) was reached from the north west and is better known today as Kensington Olympia. Services from Richmond to Kensington were withdrawn on 4th June 1916. The Kensington line formed a junction with the Hammersmith & City at Grove Road in 1870, and with the Metropolitan District Railway (MDR) east of Shaftesbury Road (now Ravenscourt

Inside, even in July 1965, South Acton still retained some distant air of its old wood-panelled elegance – and gas lamps.

Wooden platforms, crumbling brick buildings and, in 1965 even, a resolute pre-war air – note the old GENTLEMEN sign for instance. The line looks thoroughly done for here, but it was still a vital freight link, one that London (not perfectly equipped in this regard by any means) sorely needed.

Park) in 1877. It is the route from Ravenscourt Park which is used today by the District Line of London Underground, whose trains share the Railtrack route from Gunnersbury into Richmond.

Connecting Lines
1: The Metropolitan District Railway (South Acton - Acton Town)
A junction (known as District Line Junc-tion) was opened with the MDR on 15th May 1899, just north of South Acton sta-tion, to connect with the new line through Mill Hill Park. A passenger service from South Acton to Mill Hill Park (renamed Acton Town on 1st March 1910) was in-troduced on 13th June 1900. The junc-tion was not used by passenger trains and was removed in 1915. The passen-ger service between the two stations con-tinued from a separate platform, how-ever, as part of the District Railway.

2: The Midland & South Western Junction Railway (Cricklewood - Acton Wells)
Keen to get in on the act of serving west London, The Midland & South Western Junction Railway (M&SWJR) opened its 3¾ mile Cricklewood to Acton Wells line

The unprepossessing station environs at South Acton in 1965 – weeds growing up through old milk crates. It is rather sobering to realise now just how degraded we were prepared to see railway lines such as these. Closed and long-abandoned country stations often did not look as bad as this – abandoned siding, rotten woodwork, broken drainpipes. Horrible.

on 1st October 1868. The Midland Railway began operating services from Bedford to St. Pancras on the same day. Whilst this route was promoted under the M&SWJR title, it should not be confused with the railway of the same name which operated from Andover in Hampshire to Andoversford, near Cheltenham in Gloucestershire. The company referred to in this section was absorbed by the Midland Railway (MR) in 1875.

The M&SWJR left the Midland main line between Welsh Harp and Child's Hill stations, where it formed a junction. Welsh Harp opened in May 1870 (and closed in July 1903) while Child's Hill opened on 2nd May 1870. This station is today better known as Cricklewood. The southern chord line was added in 1875 to form a triangular junction. In 1871, the line was leased by the LNWR, MR and NLR. Passenger services began on 3rd August 1875, when the MR introduced eleven trains in each direction to and from Richmond. These operated as follows: 1 from Kentish Town, 7 from Moorgate Street and 3 from Childs Hill.

Two intermediate stations were opened on the line for the start of passenger operations at Willesden & Dudden Hill (renamed Dudding Hill shortly after opening) and Harrow Road. Sadly, these services were not a great success and timetable revisions took place on 1st January 1876. A month later, the service was altered to become a branch line service from Childs Hill to Harrow Road, serving Dudding Hill en route.

Further revisions took place on 1st May 1878, when the MR introduced through services from St. Pancras to Earls Court via South Acton and Turnham Green with all trains serving the two intermediate stations. Again, the service was less than successful and reductions were made in June 1880, with the line operating as a branch from Child's Hill once more. Harrow Road was renamed Stonebridge Park (not to be confused with the station of the same name on the Euston - Watford local line) on 1st July 1884. This service was withdrawn in July 1888 and both intermediate stations were closed.

It was not until 1st May 1893 that passenger services were attempted once more and these operated initially as branch trains from Child's Hill, with both intermediate stations reopened. (Stonebridge Park was later renamed Harlesden.) From January 1894, the service was extended to Gunnersbury. These services were withdrawn on 1st October 1902 and the stations closed, never to reopen.

After the withdrawal of local passenger services the line continued to serve for goods traffic as well as some through passenger workings. It remains in use today for goods and is available as a diversionary route for passenger trains. There are plans to reopen the line during the next few years and electrify it for a service to and from St. Pancras to Heathrow Airport (see Chapter 17).

3: The Great Central Railway (Neasden Junction - Brent South Junction (on the Cricklewood - Acton Wells line)

The approach of the Great Central Railway (GCR) towards the capital in the 1890s meant the virtual completion of London's rail network north of the Thames. The GC was keen to build a junction with the NLR between West Hampstead and Finchley Road & Frognal, for access the docks but the LNWR objected strongly, and it was never built.

On 7th October 1898, with the MR and the LSWR, the GC did reach an agreement, for the construction of a short spur from its own line then nearing completion to the Cricklewood - Acton Wells line. This line, from Neasden Junction to Brent South Junction, opened on 1st October 1899. The Great Central thus gained access to the docks via the MR.

4: Great Western Railway (Acton Wells - Acton Main Line)

Opened in January 1877 for goods traffic, it was known by the Great Western Railway (GWR) as the 'Poplar Goods' line, as it allowed easy access between the GWR and the many goods depots in north and east London and to Poplar Docks itself, where the GWR built its own substantial facilities.

The line was served by a Southall - Willesden Junction (High Level) service from January 1888. Through ticketing was available from stations as far away as Windsor to a wide range of destinations, some of which required a further change after Willesden Junction. A Sunday service was introduced in the summer of 1891 and included one through working from Willesden to Taplow. These services were withdrawn after the summer of 1899.

From 1904, the GWR introduced steam railmotors onto the service from the Greenford loop, though some trains continued to serve Southall. The service was never widely used and local passenger trains were withdrawn in 1912. The line is currently used by Virgin Trains from Brighton to the north (and vice

Station yard and footbridge, July 1965.

Olympia station. The exhibition complex (now most famous, of course, for the annual CAMRA beer festival) first opened way back in the 1890s, following the success of Earls Court, opened in 1886. The vaguely art deco buildings in this picture date from 1936.

versa) which travel via Kensington Olympia on the West London Line and join the GWR main line to serve Reading, Oxford, Banbury and Birmingham. This line will also be used by the proposed St. Pancras – Heathrow service (see Chapter 17).

5: West London Railway (Willesden - Kensington)

The West London Railway began life in 1836 as the Birmingham, Bristol and Thames Junction Railway. It had assumed its West London name by 1840 but did not open until 27th May 1844. It

was built to connect the London & Birmingham Railway and the GWR with the basin of the Kensington Canal and the Thames boat traffic. Financed by both companies it was built mixed, at both the standard and the broad gauge. It ran from a point near the yet to be built

Gloriously extravagant exterior to Uxbridge Road station. When built, and through their first years, the NLR stations proclaimed their presence exuberantly.

Above. In the 'white heat of technology' decade, the day passes in desultory fashion at Acton Central, 22 July 1965. Carved in the stepladders are the words 'Traffic Dept. Acton BR (M) 23 6 64'

Below. Later that 'pleasant July day' a downpour turned it into a more familiar summer day. At least it drove the photographer under cover to record the fine ironwork and solid timber roof.

Willesden Junction to the canal basin at Kensington 2½ miles away. Although intended principally for goods traffic, a passenger service operated every 30 minutes. Patronage was poor despite the provision of stations at West London Junction (south of the current Willesden Junction station), Mitre Bridge, Shepherds Bush and Kensington. The passenger service was soon withdrawn, on 30th November 1844, as considerable operating difficulties were experienced trying to cross the GWR main line from Paddington to Reading on the 'flat' at Old Oak Common. This level crossing had to be replaced by a bridge, completed in 1860.

The line was of no great importance until it was linked with the West London Extension Railway (see section 6 below). Passenger services were reintroduced at Kensington from June 1862, although intermediate stations were not reopened. A station was opened at Uxbridge Road on 1st November 1869, close to the site of the former Shepherds Bush station, and at Wormwood Scrubs on 1st August 1871. This was renamed St. Quintin Park & Wormwood Scrubs in August 1892. The first station of this name closed on 1st November 1893, replaced the same day by a new structure to the north.

6: West London Extension Railway (Kensington - Clapham Junction)

Built on the route of the filled-in Kensington Canal (only a short portion of which remained to serve Chelsea Basin), this line was built as a joint operation and was owned by four companies. The GWR and LNWR had a third each, with the LSWR and the London, Brighton & South Coast Railway (LBSCR) each owning a sixth. It ran south from Kensington to Clapham Junction.

Opened on 2nd March 1863 it was mixed gauge (see section 5 above) with intermediate stations from the start of services, at Chelsea and Battersea. Despite the main line into Victoria being mixed gauge the GWR ran through trains (formed of standard gauge stock from the first) from Southall to Victoria from 1st April 1863. The branch to Falcon Junction was also mixed gauge. Broad gauge trains from Reading and Windsor to Victoria ran until October 1866, and from then on they were formed of standard gauge stock. In the early days the longer distance trains had the coaches detached from Paddington-bound expresses at Old Oak Common. Broad gauge goods trains continued to run to the GWR goods station at Chelsea Basin. The GWR abandoned the broad gauge in 1892, but continued using Victoria until 1915.

A service was operated jointly from the beginning by the LNWR and LBSCR, from Willesden to East Croydon. The LBSCR also operated a Kensington - West Croydon service, whilst the LSWR concentrated on a Clapham Junction - Kensington shuttle.

The LNWR introduced a service from Euston to London Bridge via Kensington in July 1865. It used the line across the old Waterloo concourse to join the South Eastern Railway (SER) at what is now Waterloo East. At that time, a line linked

Top left. Acton Central, looking a bit brighter than most of the stations on the line, on a pleasant July day in 1965. The 'corporate' look of the stations is clear to see.

Middle left. Acton Central was unusual in having one of the few level crossings to be found in London. With splendid semaphore signal and siting board two or three yards ahead peeking over the curving wall, this is a wet Churchfield Road at the north end of the station, July 1965.

the main station at Waterloo with the SER station. In 1867, the service was diverted to Cannon Street but it ceased altogether a year later. From 1875 until 1893, a service operated to Waterloo (LSWR).

A station opened at West Brompton on 1st September 1866. The Metropolitan District Railway (now served by the London Underground Wimbledon Branch of the District Line) opened three years later, in April 1869. Passengers could change here when the District Railway service from West Brompton was extended to Putney Bridge on 1st May 1880, and to Wimbledon on 3rd June 1889.

Kensington was rebuilt in 1869 with two through platforms, central passing loops and bay platforms at both the north and south ends. Following the reconstruction work, Kensington was renamed Kensington (Addison Road), the name of an adjacent street and not the one on which the station actually stands! The LSWR service from Richmond (see Chapter 2) terminated in the north bay and the service from Clapham Junction at the south bay. The main platforms were used by through express trains and by services from Victoria to Southall (GWR) and from Clapham Junction to Willesden Junction (LNWR). The LNWR intro-

Acton Town 8 November 1958, car No.4176 leaving for South Acton. Photograph H.C. Casserley.

The sign on the wall in Churchfield Road read PASSENGERS MAY CROSS UNDER THE LINE BY THESE STAIRS. You'd do that if the gates were shut but it was the usual unappetising prospect. Prison-like under the gas lamps, in that Victorian 'Asylum-style' this is Acton Central on 22 July 1965.

duced a service from Broad Street to Kensington in September 1867. This was later extended to the LBSCR platforms at Victoria.

The arrival of the railway at Kensington brought about the development of the area around the station, and large town houses were built to accommodate business folk and their families.

From 1872, Kensington (Addison Road) was served by both the middle and outer circle lines, which operated in conjunction with the underground companies. At this time, the LNWR's Broad Street - Victoria service was diverted to Mansion House. As the section from Mansion House to Gloucester Road was 'underground', it was necessary for the LNWR to obtain locomotives which 'condensed their own steam' in the tunnel sections. This service was known as the 'Outer Circle', although the circle was not a complete one and ran at 30 minute intervals. After calling at Willesden Junction (High Level), these trains continued to Kensington (Addison Road), where they joined the line to Earls Court. Following electrification of the MDR in 1905, from Mansion House to Lillie Bridge near Kensington, the steam locomotives were changed for MDR electric ones at Earls Court and vice-versa. From 1908, services ran to and from Willesden Junction (High Level) and from March 1912 a steam shuttle service was implemented, which terminated at Earls Court. The line from Willesden Junction to Earls Court was electrified in 1914.

While some through trains existed after the withdrawal of the GWR service to Victoria in 1915, the LSWR operated a service from Kensington (Addison Road) to Clapham Junction and the LNWR its Willesden Junction - Earls

Court electric trains, which began in 1914. The line from Willesden Junction to Earls Court was electrified as part of the LNWR's 1911 electrification scheme (see Chapter 9). The LNWR also continued to operate the steam hauled Willesden Junction - Clapham Junction local service.

The building of an exhibition centre at Earls Court in 1886 created a goodly amount of additional passenger traffic, as did the opening of a similar complex at Olympia, in 1894. The current Earls Court facilities date from 1936.

Chelsea station was renamed Chelsea & Fulham in November 1902; it was to receive a healthy boost from the activities at Stamford Bridge opposite. The Stamford Bridge Athletic Ground had opened as early as 28th April 1877 and was used almost exclusively by the London Athletic Club, which held regular meetings. In 1904, the ground was purchased by Mr Gus Mears who saw its potential as a football stadium and he invited Fulham Football Club to consider it as a new home, an offer they declined. In 1905, it was decided to increase the number of football clubs in each of Divisions 1 and 2 of the Football League, from 18 to 20. It was decided early in 1905 to form a new club based at Stamford Bridge and apply for membership of the 2nd Division. The club held its first meeting on 14th March 1905 and signed its first players on 26th April, on the proviso that league status was attained. At the Football League's Annual Meeting held on 29th May 1905, Chelsea Football Club were elected into the 2nd Division without ever kicking a ball! At the end of their first season (1905/6) they finished third in the league, while the following season they finished second and were promoted

to Division 1 as runners-up. The success of the team meant large numbers of supporters and when Chelsea played fellow London teams such as Arsenal, Charlton and Tottenham Hotspur, many special trains were run to Chelsea & Fulham station.

Kensington (Addison Road) was also used for an extensive incoming milk traffic. Most of the wagons originated from the West Country and were remarshalled at Kensington for other parts of London, which included Bollo Lane, Ilford, Morden South and South Acton.

The line saw a heavy goods traffic from the outset, and was also used extensively by express passenger trains. The LNWR ran through trains from Birmingham to Dover and Queenborough to connect with ships to the Continent. The most famous train, however, was the 'Sunny South Express' which ran from Liverpool and Manchester via Birmingham to Brighton and Eastbourne. Although a joint operation between the LNWR and LBSCR, the service used corridor coaches, provided by the LNWR. LBSCR locomotives worked the train south of Willesden.

The 'Sunny South Express' was withdrawn during the early days of the First World War, and further wartime restrictions saw the withdrawal of the LNWR service from Willesden to Victoria, on 1st October 1917. Sunday services over the West London Line, by which title the line had become known, were also withdrawn, in May 1918. The line nonetheless saw extensive extra traffic during the Great War, and was widely used by troop trains en route to and from the Channel ports.

Following the Grouping in 1923, only the GWR retained its name. The Southern Railway (SR) took over the interests of the SECR, LBSCR and LSWR, whilst the LNWR passed into the newly formed London, Midland & Scottish Railway (LMS). The 'Sunny South Express' was reintroduced in 1921, continuing to run under LMS and SR ownership until the Second World War. During the 1930s the SR continued to operate the Clapham Junction - Kensington (Addison Road) service, with the LMS operating the steam hauled Willesden Junction - Clapham Junction services and the electrified Willesden Junction - Earls Court trains.

The outbreak of the Second World War had a dramatic effect on the line. As part of the general traffic restrictions imposed, the electric service from Willesden Junction to Earls Court was withdrawn, on 3rd October 1940, and on 20th October the line suffered from extensive bombing. The Willesden Junction - Clapham Junction service (operated by the LMS) was withdrawn after Battersea station was badly damaged by bombs, as were both West Brompton and Kensington (Addison Road). St Quintin Park & Wormwood Scrubs was burnt out by incendiaries and demolished soon after. Once repairs had been carried out, the SR restarted the service between Clapham Junction and Kensington (Addison Road). The intermediate stations, how-

Still-grand exterior to the station, in the 1950s.

ever, at Battersea, Chelsea & Fulham and West Brompton (West London Line platforms) never reopened. The line did see extensive wartime use, both goods and troop workings. Following the evacuation of Dunkirk in 1940, Kensington (Addison Road) was used as a control point.

Kensington (Addison Road) was renamed Kensington (Olympia) on 19th December 1946. While the Southern continued with its Clapham Junction - Ken-

sington (Olympia) shuttles, the local passenger service from Kensington (Olympia) to Willesden Junction never reopened and both intermediate stations remained firmly closed.

Following the formation of British Railways on 1st January 1948, the line came under the control of the Western Region, though it continued in use for through trains from the north and Midlands to the South Coast resorts, particularly during summer weekends.

These trains gradually dwindled over the years as holidaymakers were lured away by cheap package holidays to Spain and elsewhere.

A Motorail terminal was developed at Kensington Olympia in May 1966. Motorail allowed the long distance motorist to have their vehicle transported on the same train and arrive without the trouble of a strenuous drive. Destinations from Kensington (Olympia) included St. Austell, Fishguard and Stirling. As the

Acton Central, looking north.

British motorway network expanded, the need for these trains, sadly, diminished. In February 1970 the line passed from the control of the Western Region to the London Midland. In 1974 the Greater London Council's *London Rail Study* recommended the reopening of the line to local passenger trains and linking it, via the North London Line (NLL), to the Barking line at Gospel Oak.

InterCity, one of the business sectors set up by British Rail in 1982, began running through services as part of a cross-London marketing strategy in May 1986. Kensington Olympia station was upgraded to InterCity 'Parkway' status (Olympia is located close to both the M4 and M40 motorways) and the old Motorail site, now abandoned, was transformed to provide generous car parking space. Trains to and from Liverpool and Manchester ran via Birmingham and the West Coast main line before joining the West London Line at Willesden Junction. Three of these trains served Brighton, three the Dover Western Docks for ferries to France and one ran to Newhaven, for the Dieppe Ferry. Many people had expressed a desire for through services which avoided the turmoil of changing stations in London, with a taxi, bus or underground journey in between. The need for locomotive changes from electric to diesel and vice-versa (the WLL was no longer electrified) on sidings near Willesden Junction, in the shadow of a scrap yard, did little to encourage its use, each locomotive change taking around twenty minutes. The service did not enjoy the success that such enterprise might have expected and in May 1988 the three remaining trains which called at Kensington Olympia were diverted to travel via Reading and Oxford after traversing the WLL. Throughout this time, Network SouthEast continued to run the

peak hour only shuttle services between Kensington Olympia and Clapham Junction.

In April 1988, the West London Line was transferred from the London Midland Region to the Southern Region as part of the Channel Tunnel works being carried out at Waterloo and Battersea. A new depot for the servicing and maintenance of the Eurostar fleet was built at North Pole, opposite Old Oak Common depot and adjacent to the Paddington - Reading main line.

On 27th May 1994 North London Railways reopened the Willesden Junction - Kensington Olympia - Clapham Junction route throughout to local trains for the first time in 54 years. The Clapham Junction - Kensington Olympia service ceased the day before. This reinstated a service which had begun on the northern section of the line, 150 years to the day exactly.

The emergence of the route since that time is covered in Chapter 16.

Abandoned Schemes
1: The North Metropolitan Railway
The North Metropolitan Railway was authorised in 1866, to haul goods traffic from Ealing (GWR) to the docks, with junctions to many of the lines that it crossed. It never reached fruition, although its route appeared for several years on maps. It reappeared in 1911 as the Greater London Railway and was again rejected.

2: The Latimer Road & Acton Railway
Intended as an extension of GWR and Metropolitan Railway joint activity in the area, this company was set up by Act of Parliament on 18th August 1882. This allowed the construction of a line 2 miles 15 chains long from the Hammersmith

& City at Latimer Road to join the GWR main line near Acton (now main line) station.

Work began near Friars Place signal box and included the demolition of part of the historic Hindley House nearby. Financial difficulties soon arose and work stopped; a bridge was constructed across the NLR line, but it never carried any trains. Extensions to the Act were given in 1885, 1888, 1891, 1893 and again in 1895. The last extension required work to be completed by 18th August 1898. The scheme was finally abandoned by Act of Parliament on 30th July 1900.

Easing the bottleneck
To gain access to the lines described in this chapter, North London Line trains were adding considerably to the now-congested two track LNWR main line between Hampstead Road and what was to eventually become Willesden Junction. To solve the problem, the building of a relief line from Camden Road to the Kew and Richmond lines was planned. The result, as we shall see from the next Chapter, was the building of the Hampstead Junction Railway. It saved for the moment the expense of boring additional tunnels at Primrose Hill, though this would have to be undertaken eventually by the LNWR. The new line would open up the expanding and prosperous residential area around Hampstead Heath.

South Acton revived – sort of – in 1978, looking south. Electric lights and a new footbridge have appeared; the wooden platforms remain but the down side buildings have gone and part of the up side, too. Progress of a sort! Photograph N.D. Mundy.

The shambles at Gunnersbury. Today the scene is hardly a railway one at all and the passenger feels his train has just run into the nether regions of a multi-storey car park. The place indeed had a chequered history – it was an island platform and the building lost its roof in a storm of unusual intensity on 8 December 1954. This temporary expedient sufficed until an office block was built over the station in the 1960s.

Woodstock Road Halt on the branch line from South Acton to Hammersmith. The halt was one of three opened in 1909 when steam railmotors were introduced in an attempt to boost passenger numbers.

'Faded glory' is a theme to be met with time and again, looking at these North London stations. This is Hampstead Heath on 13 October 1950 with that gorgeous wooden relief sign and the Vaseline Hair Tonic poster – all you need for success with the opposite sex. There were always posters for Southend on the North London stations but New Brighton in the Wirral would seem to be long shot....

Chapter Three
Through Hampstead Heath

The Hampstead Junction Railway (Camden Road - Old Oak Junction)
Although promoted by the LNWR, the Hampstead Junction Railway (HJR) was a nominally independent concern, running from a junction with the NLR at Kentish Town Junction (just west of the current Camden Road station), to Old Oak Junction on the N&SWJR (see previous Chapter).

Authorised in 1853 as the North & South Western, Hampstead & City Junction Railway, the line did not open until 2nd January 1860, due to problems encountered during its construction. There were two major civil engineering structures on the route: a 94-span viaduct nearly a mile long through the (even then) heavily built up area of Kentish Town, and the 1,167 yard long Hamp-

stead Heath Tunnel, with its approach retaining walls, taking the line under open country at a depth of 160ft.

The construction of this little line seems to have been dogged by problems from the start. The acquisition of land was slow and in 1856 application was made to Parliament for an extension of the time allowed for completion. The original contractor, a Mr Hayton of Kilsby

Gospel Oak in 1965, with new building and steel shelter provided, rather in the style of some of the 1930s LT stations.

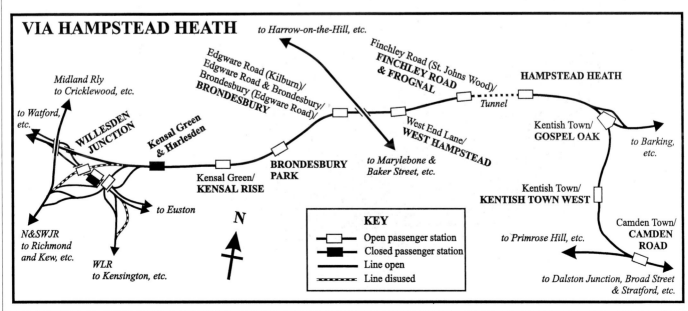

VIA HAMPSTEAD HEATH

What more eloquent justification for the rebuilding could there be than this picture of the poor old original building at Gospel Oak, 3 November 1950?

and Stamford, died and was replaced by Thomas Armstrong. The tunnel works caused problems, with the sub-contractors described 'as being of no means or responsibility'. Pressure from the clay made it necessary to use Staffordshire bricks in places, and it caused the collapse of some 70 yards on Sunday 29th August 1858. It was finally completed in June 1859, having consumed some 14 million bricks. The approaches to the tunnel were described in *The Illustrated London News* as 'of a novel character'. Just how novel is revealed by the continual trouble they have caused to successive engineers! Even then, the opening of the line was postponed several times because the signalling works were incomplete, even though at Kentish Town Junction it boasted the first use of signal and point interlocking in the world.

The opening of the line provided a 'service of 23 trains a day in each direction to Fenchurch Street' and must have given considerable relief to the two track section of the LNWR between Camden and Willesden. It would appear that both

The North London of the 1950s changed little; much of it was poor, the 'bomb site' as an institution clung doggedly on, rationing was still in force for some foods, coal was often hard to get, winters were plagued by fogs and so on. Eerily, many of the NLR – or rather, LNWR – buildings seems to capture this gloomy spirit perfectly... This is the south side of Gospel Oak station, with Gordon House Road passing underneath, 3 November 1950.

Top left. Brondesbury Park station, opened in 1908 and, if hardly a rural idyll, at least living in part up to its name, in 1979. Photograph N.D. Mundy.

Middle left. Interior of Brondesbury Park, 1979. Photograph N.D. Mundy.

Bottom left. Willesden Junction, with what must be one of the biggest 'destination' boards in British railway practice. As well as Broad Street it includes Clapham Junction, Carlisle and 'all parts of Scotland', so recent attempts to highlight the interchange opportunities along the North London lines are nothing new! The old main line booking office was for many years the focal point at this key interchange station which in reality, was three separate stations on the same site!

the line and the train service were operated by the NLR until 2nd September 1867, when a connection with the West London Line (WLL) was opened. The HJR passed into LNWR ownership and the LNWR began a service between Broad Street and Victoria via Kensington, with the NLR securing running rights from the LNWR. There were originally four stations, at Kentish Town (later Gospel Oak), Hampstead Heath, Finchley Road (St. Johns Wood) and Edgeware [sic] Road (Kilburn).

Willesden Junction

Willesden Junction station opened on 1st September 1866, to serve the Hampstead Junction line. It was not, however, the first station to serve the locality. A station in Acton Lane (later known as Willesden), was opened *circa* 1842 by the London & Birmingham Railway. Little is known about it, except that it seems to have been mainly for the personal use of Captain Mark Huish, Chairman of the LNWR (1846-1858) who lived nearby. It should be remembered that at that time, Willesden was a small village in open country.

The new station became a major interchange. Main line platforms were provided and these linked two high level stations. Platforms serving Hampstead and Richmond were located at the north end, whilst those serving Earls Court and Kensington were at the south end (opened 2nd September 1867). Both high level stations had services to Broad Street, which caused much confusion, not to mention annoyance, to the passengers and it was not unknown for them to be seen wandering between the two high level stations looking for trains! This problem was solved on 20th July 1885, when a new line, the Kew Curve was opened, connecting the Kensington platforms with Acton Wells Junction, thus allowing all the east-west services to be concentrated there. The Kew platforms at the south end were taken out of use at the same time, although the line through the former north end high level station continued in use for goods traffic until 1st May 1892. The old junction at Old Oak was then removed and replaced by a connection to Kew Curve, and other major work took place.

A new line was built for use by all Up

Top left. Willesden Junction High Level platform looking east. The footpath on the left still exists, linking the station with Harrow Road, though the Oerlikon unit is of course but a distant memory. An Engineer's train stands in the former bay platform (No.10).

Middle left. A footbridge linked the main line island platform on the high level lines with the Kensington line platform opposite. This is the island platform, looking east.

Bottom left. A view eastwards on 24 March 1953 with the old Kensington line platform on the right, which has become disused. It was served mainly by electric trains to and from Kensington Olympia.

Broad Street trains, with a new bridge over the LNWR main line, an island platform and a new station at Willesden Junction High Level. The old Kensington lines remained to serve Down trains from Broad Street. At the same time, the old Kew line bridge was removed, although one abutment can still be found near the old Area Manager's office. The abutment on the other side of the line was only removed in the 1970s, when a new factory was built. The work was completed for the new lines to be opened on 12th August 1894.

Station Openings and Renamings

When the Hampstead Junction Railway opened in 1860, stations were provided at Kentish Town, Hampstead Heath, Finchley Road (St. Johns Wood) and Edgware [sic] Road (Kilburn). Kentish Town station was renamed Gospel Oak on 1st February 1867, pending the opening of a new station closer by. The new Kentish Town station opened two months later. Kensal Green & Harlesden opened on 1st November 1861. The original staggered platforms are still visible today.

'Edgeware Road (Kilburn)' station was renamed Edgware Road & Brondesbury on 1st January 1872, but this was short-lived, for a year later it was renamed Brondesbury (Edgware Road). Kensal Green & Harlesden was replaced by a new Kensal Green station on 1st July 1873. Finchley Road (St. Johns Wood) was renamed Finchley Road & Frognal on 1st October 1880, whilst Brondesbury (Edgware Road) became plain Brondesbury on 1st May 1883. A new station opened at West End Lane on 1st March 1888. Brondesbury Park station opened on 1st June 1908.

Accident at Hampstead Heath

Hampstead Heath became a popular destination for many Londoners. On the Heath they could walk in the open park and enjoy the fresh air, a luxury not available to many of them in a heavily industrialised and polluted city. It became so busy on Sundays that the station was frequently overcrowded. *The Hampstead & Highgate Express* (23rd April 1892) reported that over 100,000 visited the Heath on Easter Monday (18th April) to enjoy the activities, ranging from pony and donkey riding to the steam roundabouts.

After 5pm, the sky on the Heath became very overcast, prompting many visitors to suddenly change their plans and set about returning home. The newspaper reporter described some of those making for the station as 'uncontrolled boisterous holiday-makers'. The ticket inspectors stood in boxes at the bottom of the footbridge steps, which did little to assist in rapid dispersal of the crowds along the length of the platforms. As a result, a considerable backlog of people assembled both on the footbridge and the steps leading from it, awaiting access to the platforms themselves. Shortly after the departure of the 6.2pm Down train, the right-hand side of the station footbridge collapsed and in the ensuing panic, a major disaster unfolded. Six children and two women lost their lives, with many people sustaining serious injuries.

Following the accident, the LNWR Board was severely criticised. The Chairman of the Hampstead Board of Guardians claimed that as the NLR was 90% owned by the LNWR, the LNWR was therefore responsible for the accommodation at the station being wholly inadequate. The inquest was opened on Thursday 21st April 1892, and reconvened on Tuesday 26th April. Considerable reference was made in the newspaper reports to *'alterations made in 1881, including the erection of gates and tickets barriers and to correspondence between the Hampstead Vestry, the LNWR and the Board of Trade, regarding the perceived dangers of these installations'.* The LNWR Engineer, Francis Stevenson, was required to give evidence on the second day and agreed to a request from the Coroner 'to remove the ticket collecting boxes from the bottom of the staircases'.

The cause of death was given as 'suffocation' and an 'accidental' verdict was recorded. In addition to the relocation of the ticket boxes, the LNWR had to review its Bank holiday arrangements and instigate better crowd control procedures during periods of heavy use. This led to the building of a ramp to the Up platform for excursion and Bank Holiday traffic. When the station was rebuilt in 1954, this feature was retained, although it was no longer used.

East to West

The NLR was now able to operate services from east London to west London and

Top right. **Little shelter is provided on the now disused Kensington line platform – much of the boarding, indeed, has been removed. Services between Willesden Junction and Kensington Olympia were withdrawn in 1940.**

Middle right. **Willesden Junction in 1965 (rebuilding took place in 1956/57) looking east from the footpath leading to Harrow Road.**

Bottom right. **Willesden High Level Booking Office in July 1965. It served those passengers arriving at the station from Harrow Road via the footpath. After a period out of use, this entrance, suitably refurbished, was reopened in 1996.**

Top right. Kensal Rise on Chamberlayne Road, in the north London rain, 22 July 1965. Originally known as Kensal Green and Harlesden, it became Kensal Rise from 24 May 1890.

Middle right. The station yard at Kensal Rise (Chamberlayne Road runs left to right ahead) on 22 July 1965. The cars are sad indicators of the times – a foreign bubble car and three of the consummately awful 'beetles'.

Bottom right. Down on the platforms at Kensal Rise in July 1965 – thoroughly straightforward and highly typical LNWR style.

Surrey. While it had its uses as a cross London orbital railway, the Directors began to realise the missed opportunity of not having a London terminus of its own. It was a situation that would soon be rectified, as we shall see in the next chapter.

Connecting Lines
Although it was originally intended for The Tottenham & Hampstead Junction Railway (TH&JR) to join up with the Hampstead Junction Railway at Gospel Oak, lack of funds resulted in the first attempt being abandoned. Although resurrected in the 1880s, the LNWR and NLR were less than enthusiastic about the project, hence the need for the T&HJR to build its own station next to the existing facilities at Gospel Oak. It was not until the First World War that a physical connection was finally achieved. These efforts, therefore, justify the inclusion of this route in this account.

The Tottenham & Hampstead Junction Railway (South Tottenham - Highgate Road, later extended to Gospel Oak)
The Tottenham & Hampstead Railway was incorporated in 1862, to construct a line four miles in length from Tottenham, on the GER London - Cambridge line, to Highgate Road, a quarter of a mile east of Gospel Oak station. The original intention was to provide facilities at Gospel Oak, allowing interchange with the Hampstead Junction Railway. Work commenced on the station and a well for a locomotive turntable, but stopped in June 1868, due to shortage of funds. In 1870, the works were demolished and the turntable well covered in.

The line opened between Tottenham and Highgate Road on 21st July 1868 and was used initially by GER trains from Fenchurch Street. To reach the Tottenham & Hampstead route, trains had to reverse at Tottenham station (now known as Tottenham Hale), joining the new line at Tottenham North Junction. There were just two intermediate stations on the line to begin with, at Crouch Hill and Upper Holloway. The terminus at Highgate Road would eventually become a through station, known as Highgate Road High Level after the opening of the adjacent Low Level facilities in 1900.

The service did not prove popular, however, and services were withdrawn on

Hampstead Heath, a fairly grim place, 13 October 1950. The days are long gone when the station dealt with vast crowds at bank holidays and some summer weekends – in the 1890s 100,000 Londoners might visit the Heath on an Easter Monday.

31st January 1870. The company was soon in financial difficulty but closure was only short-lived, as the Midland Railway had come to its rescue by constructing a connection from its main line at Kentish Town. The MR began operating passenger trains from Moorgate Street from 1st October 1870, initially to Crouch Hill and later to South Tottenham & Stamford Hill, once this station had been built. This allowed the MR and the GER to exchange traffic, the MR gaining access to London Docks and the GER access to St. Pancras. A number of additional passenger stations opened, including South Tottenham & Stamford Hill 1st May 1871. Hornsey Road and Junction Road both opened on 1st Janu-

ary 1872. A further station opened at Green Lanes on 1st June 1880 and St Ann's Road completed the network on 2nd October 1882. Highgate Road (High Level) closed in 1915, whilst Hornsey Road, Junction Road and St. Ann's Road would all become casualties of the Second World War .

In 1887, the decision was taken to resurrect the original formation into Gospel Oak. Opened on 4th June 1888, the line finally reached Gospel Oak. Neither the LNWR nor the NLR would allow the Tottenham & Hampstead a physical connection with the Hampstead Junction Railway. This resulted in a single platform with modest facilities being built adjacent to the main station, for

GER trains terminating from Chingford. This platform remained in use until September 1926, when it was closed to regular passenger traffic, though it was available for excursions until 7th August 1939. A new platform would eventually be built on a slightly different alignment in 1981, to accommodate the Barking trains (see Chapter 15).

A connection was provided at South Tottenham with the GER's Enfield branch at Seven Sisters Junction. This route opened to passenger traffic on 1st January 1880 and was used mainly by trains between North Woolwich and Palace Gates. Since withdrawal of this service in 1963, this connecting line has been

The even grimmer booking hall at Hampstead Heath, with its hideous blocked off office ('BOOK HERE' crudely hand-written in chalk) on 13 October 1950. In a sudden Easter Monday downpour, as the text relates, a horrible accident took place. Passengers rushing for the train ('uncontrolled boisterous holiday-makers' according to the local paper) led to the collapse of the right-hand side of the station footbridge. In the panic six children and two women were killed, and many others injured.

Tidied up to look almost bonny, Hampstead Heath station in August 1965. Di Palma's greengrocers is still there, though it has moved with the times as necessary, becoming more of a general grocery – compare with the main picture at the head of this chapter. A new booking office was provided in 1968.

used for freight and empty stock workings. It is electrified at 25 kV through South Tottenham station before connecting with the Stratford line at Tottenham South Junction.

In the 1880s a further connecting line was built, from Harringay Park Junction to the GNR main line at Harringay. Although most of the work was carried out, the line was not joined to the GNR system and was eventually lifted a few years later. The First World War was responsible for its completion, the line opening in May 1916 for goods traffic. In

more recent times, it was used by InterCity for empty stock workings of High Speed Trains (HSTs) between Bounds Green Depot and St. Pancras. Since privatisation, Bounds Green has been responsible for maintenance of the Great North Eastern Railway (GNER) fleet and main line services to and from St. Pancras have been operated by Midland Main Line, which are now maintained at Derby and elsewhere.

The MR opened its own facilities at South Tottenham & Stamford Hill in 1871 and at Upper Holloway around the

same time. Goods facilities were provided at Green Lanes in 1880. In 1886, the GER opened a large goods depot at Tufnell Park to serve the Metropolitan Cattle Market. All goods yards were closed between 1964 and 1968.

A further connecting line was built from Mortimer Street Junction to Engine Shed Junction, Kentish Town, opening for traffic on 17th December 1900. A station, known as Highgate Road Low Level, opened with it and remained until closure on 1st March 1918. The two stations were linked by a connecting footbridge.

Hampstead Heath, rebuilt in unsympathetic (let's be honest – downright awful) style, 4 May 1953. It has subsequently been demolished and replaced in a more agreeable style.

Finchley Road & Frognal, obviously closely akin to the Hampstead Heath station building and faintly art deco, 1 September 1965. Typical of the age – a mini-van with dent in the back.

The High Level station closed on 1st October 1915. The Low Level line remains to this day for freight use. The Tottenham & Hampstead passed into the joint ownership of the MR and GER in 1902.

The Tottenham & Forest Gate Railway (South Tottenham - Woodgrange Road)

In 1894, the MR joined forces with the LT&SR to build a six mile long line from South Tottenham & Stamford Hill, to join with the original LTS line from Forest Gate Junction (between Forest Gate and Manor Park stations) to Tilbury via Barking. The LTS had opened the Tilbury line on 13th April 1854, with a station at Barking on the same day, served by trains operating to and from Bishopsgate and Fenchurch Street.

The line beyond South Tottenham & Stamford Hill opened to traffic on 9th July 1894. Stations were provided from the start at Black Horse Road, Walthamstow, Leyton, Leytonstone and Wanstead Park to traditional MR architectural design, whilst the LT&SR was responsible for building Woodgrange Park, on its original line through Barking. The building of this line enabled the MR to run through services to Southend and Tilbury Docks and for the LT&SR to serve St. Pancras. On the same day a connecting line opened from Woodgrange Park to East Ham, where some passenger trains terminated. After rebuilding in 1905, a bay platform was provided at East Ham for this service.

Beyond Walthamstow the line climbed, to run on viaduct high above the areas it served. In November 1890, the MR agreed proposed sites for goods facilities at Black Horse Road, Boundary Road (opened as Queens Road, Walthamstow), Hainault Road (opened as Leyton) and Royal Lodge (opened as Leytonstone). The LT&SR was responsible for building the goods facilities at Woodgrange Park. Like the facilities provided on the Tottenham & Hampstead all were to close between 1964 and 1968. Both these lines were wholly owned by the MR from 1912.

A Through Route

The building of both the Tottenham and Hampstead and the Tottenham & Forest Gate Railways eventually provided a useful orbital route, although it was to take the First World War to maximise the potential of its various connections. From the 1960s until 1981, diesel multiple units operated between Kentish Town and Barking. Today, Silverlink Trains operate passenger services between Gospel Oak and Barking – details can be found in later chapters. The line is also being used again for freight traffic, after a period confined to passenger use.

Finchley Road & Frognal – the usual LNWR canopies, 1 September 1965.

The wonderful confection that was Broad Street station. A measure of its importance, which declined to vanishing point, is that it once served more passengers than almost all the other London termini, apart from Liverpool Street and Victoria. Opened in 1865, it was a sumptuous outcome to a line which had begun as a link from the London & Birmingham Railway to the London Docks. The two 'three legged' covered footbridges were added during rearrangements of the interior completed in 1890. Photograph National Railway Museum.

Chapter Four
The Happy Afterthought

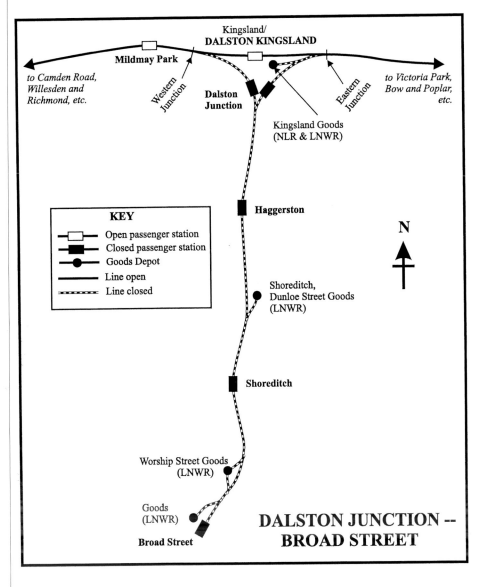

KEY

☐	Open passenger station
■	Closed passenger station
●	Goods Depot
——	Line open
┅┅	Line closed

Kingsland/
DALSTON KINGSLAND

Mildmay Park

to Camden Road,
Willesden and
Richmond, etc.

Western Junction

Dalston Junction

Eastern Junction

to Victoria Park,
Bow and Poplar,
etc.

Kingsland Goods
(NLR & LNWR)

N

Haggerston

Shoreditch,
Dunloe Street Goods
(LNWR)

Shoreditch

Worship Street Goods
(LNWR)

Goods
(LNWR)

Broad Street

DALSTON JUNCTION --
BROAD STREET

A Terminus of Its Own

It soon became apparent that the NLR required a city terminus of its own, rather than Fenchurch Street which was reached on the circuitous route via Bow. Fenchurch Street was becoming busier and difficulties were emerging over the scheduling of NLR services into and out of the terminus. The only way forward was for the Directors of the NLR to build their own City terminus, a decision afterwards referred to as the 'Happy Afterthought'! They were also anxious to provide goods facilities within the City of London itself. The NLR Directors accordingly obtained the agreement of the LNWR Board for a Parliamentary Bill to be deposited, which was achieved by the NLR borrowing £40,000 from the LNWR and £20,000 from its bankers. The City Extension, therefore, became a joint operation and as a result, an Act of Parliament got the Royal Assent in July 1861, to construct a line from a point near Kingsland to a City terminus at Liverpool Street, named after Lord Liverpool who was Prime Minister 1812-1827. The LNWR contributed half the costs to build the upper passenger terminal and paid for the entire goods facilities beneath it – eventually it paid far more than the NLR did! This terminus became known as Broad Street, after the nearby road of that name.

The Eastern Counties Railway (ECR) was also looking for a city terminus and asked the NLR for facilities at its proposed new station. They were refused and this decision resulted in the ECR later building the adjacent Liverpool Street station. During the Parliamentary process for the extension of the ECR line

The front of the station, doubtless photographed from a point up on the roof. Like Liverpool Street below and to the right, the intensive service run by small tank engines needed little coal stages at many of the platform ends; Broad Street had four of these and there were a further lengthy pair of stages further out. The wagons are there to top up one of these latter stages. The end of platform stages looked exactly like the one visible down at Platforms 4 and 5, in Liverpool Street station. Photograph National Railway Museum.

The great open halls of Broad Street in 1898, when the North London Railway conducted a photographic survey of much of its estate. The roof cleaning/repair rig over Platform 1 and 2 was an ingenious arrangement which moved forward by placing sleeper timbers fitted longitudinally with rails one in front of the other. Note the engine pits running the length of the platform roads. These ran the full length of Platforms 1-4 but were restricted by the crossovers at the buffer ends to Platforms 5-8. Photograph National Railway Museum.

from Bishopsgate to Liverpool Street, one of the principal objectors was the NLR!

Construction Begins
Building the 2 mile 22 chain line from Dalston to Broad Street was neither easy or cheap. Housing in London in the 1860s was tightly packed and the approach line through Haggerston and Shoreditch, and the terminus itself, made for a great deal of demolition. The need for land purchase to be kept to a minimum forced the company to build the line on a viaduct for most of its length. While nearby Bishopsgate contained some elegant and historic buildings, the housing which then existed in the area adjacent to the new terminus was of poor quality. The result was a major 'slum' clearance exercise. While most welcomed the removal of substandard property, many of the residents

Platforms 3 and 4 in 1898. This eastern part was the 'North London' side, the western side being devoted to the LNWR.

The 'LNW' side at Broad Street, 1898. The carriage boards read BROAD ST WILLESDEN KENSINGTON & MANSION HOUSE CHANGE AT WILLESDEN FOR MAIN LINE.

combined to form a petition, which Lord Derby presented (unsuccessfully) to the House of Lords in February 1864. The £1.2m cost of the project was high by the standards of the 1860s. £307,000 was expended purchasing property from some 242 different land owners. A further £11,000 had to be paid in compensation to those made homeless. Around 640 houses had to be demolished before Broad Street station could be built, the population reducing from 12,000 to 8,000 as a result. Demolition work included removal of almost 400 skeletons from Bethlehem Hospital (Bedlam) Burial Ground. A condition of building the line was that the company would provide cheap workmen's trains from Dalston Junction to Broad Street, for those inconvenienced by its building.

The City Extension was built with three tracks from Dalston to Broad Street, constructed mainly on viaducts. Before the line opened, an agreement was

Broad Street's heyday came early and its passenger traffic was already on the wane before the Great War. Electric trains were thought to be the salvation and they began running to Richmond in 1916.

Huddle and muddle at Broad Street in July 1957. Traffic had dropped to embarrassing levels by this time, so that BR closed off the main block altogether. The buildings under construction would be the new stationmaster's office and booking office, completed that year.

reached between the NLR and LNWR regarding the conveying of goods to and from the city – the LNWR to carry all the goods traffic, with the NLR charged at cost. As first built the station had seven platforms, although later there were eight, and from 1913, nine. Broad Street roof and the viaducts on which it stood were designed by the LNWR's Chief Engineer, William Baker, once assistant to Robert Stephenson. It is likely, however, that the architectural refinements of Baker's design were carried out by J. Stainsby, also of the LNWR. Baker's plans had to be revised in 1863, when it was decided to set the main station en-

trance back from the main road (Liverpool Street). The station was lengthened at the north end as part of the scheme. The Contractor was Holland & Harrison, working under the direction of Lewis Cubitt, and work suffered from several delays, including a strike among the workmen.

Broad Street Opens
Broad Street station was officially opened on 31st October 1865, by the Lord Mayor of London, passenger services commencing the following day. The effect was both immediate and dramatic, with passenger figures doubling throughout

the NLR empire. The passenger station built above the goods depot made for a high, imposing building, with wagons raised and lowered on lifts. The LNWR opened its goods facilities on 18th May 1868. There was soon a reorganisation of trackwork and platforms, in 1876. The platform on the eastern side (nearest the GER's Liverpool Street station, opened in 1874) was designated No.1. From the start of services, on 1st November 1865, NLR trains ran four times each hour to both Chalk Farm and Bow, and twice an hour to Kew.

Station Openings and Closures
The opening of the City Extension saw new stations at Shoreditch and Dalston Junction, allowing closure of Kingsland station (see Chapter 1) which, once Broad Street had opened, sat at the base of the triangle on a line no longer used by passenger trains. The new Dalston Junction was located at the southern apex of the triangular junction, giving access to services to and from Broad Street and destinations both east and the west. The final station on the City Extension, Haggerston, opened on 2nd September 1867.

Service Alterations
From the opening of Broad Street in October 1865, a service ran from Broad Street to Fenchurch Street via Bow. This was reduced from 1st August 1866, when services were extended south of Bow, over previously goods only lines, to Poplar. A further extension to Blackwall (the original eastern terminus of the London & Blackwall) opened for traffic on 1st September 1870. These trains ran non-stop from Poplar (NLR) station to Blackwall, despite passing through the London &

Gloom at Broad Street, 16 June 1950 – the air of decline is palpable. Liverpool Street station is visible through the opening.

Blackwall's own Poplar station. Local services which had previously operated out of Fenchurch Street to Kew and Willesden via Hampstead Heath were diverted to Broad Street following the opening of the terminus. Now with its own city terminus, the NLR ceased operating out of Fenchurch Street on 31st December 1868. These services were replaced by a GER shuttle from Fenchurch Street to Bow, on 1st January 1869.

Connecting Lines

On 18th May 1869, the line from Bow to the London, Tilbury & Southend Railway (LT&SR) was opened, thus allowing the NLR to operate through excursion trains from Broad Street to the Thames ports and Southend. The main service on this route was a shuttle from Bow to Plaistow.

LNWR Services Begin

A service to Watford was introduced by the LNWR in September 1866. A year later one to Kensington (Addison Road) was introduced and this was then extended to Victoria (LBSCR). This arrangement continued until 1871, when installation of Earls Court Junction, just south of Addison Road station, offered access to the Metropolitan District Railway.

Trains no longer reached Victoria via Clapham Junction but ran instead via Earls Court (MDR), continuing along the southern side of what we now know as the Circle Line to Mansion House, where a platform was rented by the LNWR as its terminus. This was marketed as the 'outer circle', in contrast to the 'inner circle', today known simply as the Circle Line. The service was cut back to Earls Court in 1909, following electrification of the MDR. Further details can be found in Chapter 9.

Main Line Services Introduced

The LNWR also inaugurated services from Broad Street to stations on its main line. New 50ft. coaches were built in 1900, for the Broad Street - Watford services. When the 'New Line' was completed from Willesden Junction to Watford High Street early in 1913, the Euston - Watford semi-fast service was run on that line, instead of the existing slow line. By 1896, one train a day ran between Broad Street and Tring which, by 1909, had been increased to four Down and two Up workings per day. At the same time, capacity released on the slow lines was used to extend the Broad street semi-fast service beyond Watford to Tring. The posters issued in 1913, promoting the 'North Western Country Services', included the suburban service from Watford to Tring.

By now, the LNWR's London to Birmingham route was under threat from the new direct line being built by the GWR. Running from Northolt Junction to Aynho Junction near Banbury, via High Wycombe, this line opened on 1st July 1910, allowing the GWR to considerably reduce its journey time from Paddington to Snow Hill. The LNWR responded to the threat by commencing a new service, 'The City to City Express', from Broad Street to Wolverhampton via Birmingham New Street, from 1st February 1910, four months before the new GWR service began. An early inter-city service, it was aimed principally at the business traveller, who was able to have letters or reports typed up en-route! The Up train ran in the morning and the Down train in the evening as follows right. All trains between Broad Street and Tring and vice-versa travelled via Chalk Farm.

Coping With Demand

To cope with increased traffic, the lines from Dalston Western Junction to Camden Road were quadrupled (see Chapter 1) becoming available for traffic in May 1871. A fourth track was added from Dalston Junction to Haggerston in December 1872 and in July

Broad Street, 16 June 1950. The station was reduced to a poor hovel indeed in the late 1960s, when the roof, in need of repairs, was taken off and simple awnings substituted. It was a curious experience to walk out into the wide spaces where a single growling DMU sat in the sun waiting for the off to Finsbury Park and the distant northern suburbs.

Up train		
Wolverhampton	depart	7.45 am
Dudley Port	depart	7.55
Smethick	depart	8.06
Birmingham N. St.	arrive	8.15
	depart	8.20
Coventry	depart	8.43
Willesden Jct. did not stop on outward journey		
Broad Street	arrive	10.35

Down train		
Broad Street	depart	5.25 pm
Willesden Jct.	depart	5.44 *
Coventry	arrive	7.17
Birmingham N. St.	arrive	7.40
Smethick did not stop on inward journey		
Dudley Port did not stop on inward journey		
Wolverhampton	arrive	8.05

*Allowed connections off the 5.20 pm from Euston and 5.20 pm from Kensington (Addison Road)

In February 1913, trains left Tring for Broad Street (arrival times in brackets) at:

Tring	depart	8.16 am(arrive 9.22)
Tring	depart	8.46 (arrive 9.50).

In the evening, Tring services left Broad Street (arrival times in brackets) at:

Broad Street	depart	4.20 pm(arrive 5.40)
Broad Street	depart	5.02 (arrive 6.06)
Broad Street	depart	6.04 (arrive 7.12).

1874, it was extended to Broad Street itself, apart from the bridge over Great Eastern Street, which was not completed

Looking out through the station approach at the 'LNW' side, 16 June 1950.

until two years later. Because this fourth track was principally for fast trains, neither Haggerston nor Shoreditch stations were provided with platforms to serve it.

Additional Goods Facilities
Around 1874, further goods premises were provided at Worship Street, but it was not long before the LNWR required more room to deal with its goods traffic on the city extension, in order to relieve Broad Street. It undertook a survey of

suitable sites in 1889, before deciding to place new facilities between Cremer Street and Pearson Street, near Shoreditch. The goods depot was located between Pearson Street and Dunloe Street with tracks at both rail and street level, connected by hydraulic lifts. A coal depot was built between Dunloe Street and Cremer Street, with sidings at the higher level. The coal was emptied over chutes and dropped to the storage bins below, to be put on to carts for onward

transit. Building these depots required the demolition of the old signal box on the Up side and its replacement by the new Dunloe Street signal box on the Down side.

Broad Street - London's Third Busiest Terminus
In 1890, Broad Street was so busy that two footbridge staircases had to be built from street level to each side of the concourse, to ease the problems of crowding

Dalston Junction box stood at the south end of the station, at the end of platforms 2 and 3 (Dalston Junction had six platforms). In this view, looking towards Broad Street, the lines from Poplar emerge from the left, the electrified lines (platforms 1 and 2 are on the right while the non-electrified lines to Dalston Western Junction are in the centre.

in getting in and out of the place. In 1891, an eighth platform was added and the station was at its busiest, with over three million passengers a year. The Underground had yet to penetrate the NLR heartland and the effects of tramways and omnibuses had yet to be felt. In 1898, 71 trains arrived and departed from Broad Street between 9 and 10 am. Broad Street was the third busiest of London's termini, handling almost 800 train arrivals/departures per day. Of its contemporaries, only Liverpool Street and Victoria exceeded these numbers.

Interchange at Broad Street was further improved in 1912, when the Central London Railway (CLR) extended its underground line (now the Central Line) from Bank to Liverpool Street. An entrance was provided at ground level in front of the station, and a CLR booking office was provided on the Broad Street concourse. A ninth platform was built in 1913, on the western (LNWR) side. Some improvements were also made to the concourse and footbridges and new facade was built, in Portland Stone, at the same time. There was coal and water for locomotives working into the station, at various points on the station approaches, and access was gained across various crossovers and junctions.

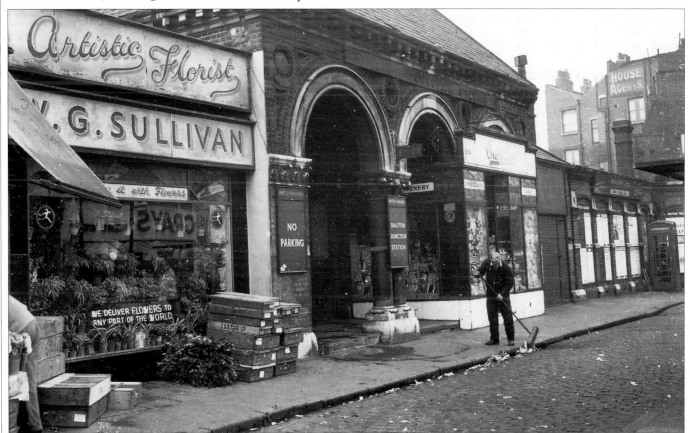

Top and above. The line down to Broad Street began in the curiously isolated district of Dalston, looked down upon as 'rough' even by the near-destitute inhabitants of Finsbury Park. W.G. Sullivan, unlikely enough, promises to deliver flowers 'to any part of the world'.

Above. Period cameo.

Below. Bow Junction, about 1871. Prior to 1884 the engine shed – note the water columns and so on – was actually in the works. Photograph National Railway Museum.

Chapter Five
The Railway Town in the City

Land Purchase and Early Work
At the Board meeting of the E&WIDBJR (to remind ourselves – the East & West India Docks & Birmingham Junction Railway) on 30th December 1846, it was reported that George Weston had communicated with the company and 'required them to purchase the whole of his estate in the Parish of St Mary le Bow'. The Board referred the matter to the Solicitor. At the meeting on 5th May 1847, it was reported that 'a cheque' had duly been paid to Mr Weston. At that time the company often had to purchase land in excess of what it required, aiming to sell it on later if it was not needed for operational requirements – sometimes this was not until many years later.

The line through Bow was the first to advance. We know that on 2nd August 1847, the E&WIDBJR Board had received ten tenders for the construction of the section of line from the Lea Cut to Sheppard Lane. The contract was awarded to Thomas Jackson, who had submitted a construction price of £39,472.

Early Days
From the opening of the line, locomotives and rolling stock were supplied by the LNWR – this was reported to the Meeting of Proprietors held on 25th February 1851. LNWR locomotive arrangements at that time included a roundhouse on the east side of the line at Camden and a straight shed and repair shed opposite. It was the intention of the Directors to hire in all locomotives and rolling stock and not become an independently operated company. At the Meeting of Proprietors held on 24th February 1852, the sum of £7,710 15/- 10d was recorded as paid to the LNWR for hire of locomotives. Carriage repairs were recorded at £467 14/- 3d. This situation was not to last for long.

Change of Name and Policy
The Meeting of Proprietors held on 17th June 1853 agreed that the name of the company should be changed to the North London Railway (NLR). The meeting, however, was principally concerned with increasing the capital of the company and in the issue of additional shares. Part of the requirement for the increased capital was to enable the company to *procure suitable plant of engines and carriages, with the necessary workshops and other conveniences which are found to be required…*' Those present heard that *'when the company was first projected, it was not contemplated that it would be worked independently, neither, indeed, was it expected that passenger traffic would form so important a portion of the company's business, consequently, no provision was made in the original capital for the purchase of land required. In the present time, the locomotives, and a great portion of the carriages have been hired. Much em-barrassment has resulted from this system – the stock (especially locomotives) after trial, it has been ascertained to be ill adapted to the peculiar traffic, and, it is believed that considerable saving may be effected by the arrangement now being contemplated'.*

The proprietors acceded to this 'arrangement' – something which was to make a considerable mark on the Bow area and the development of the company in general.

Establishing a Railway Town
It was normal for railway companies to establish their workshops in fresh fields, close to a village which might then be dramatically expanded. Familiar examples are Crewe, Swindon, Melton Constable and Wolverton. Around the shops the company built houses and also provided the schools, churches and the inevitable Railway Institute, for the improvement of the workers. Bow proved something of an exception to this, for the NLR was an urban creature, and simply utilised the land it owned around the existing village community. Bow did, however, get its Railway Institute, in 1869.

The Locomotive Superintendents
With the decision to opt for independent operation, one of the first tasks was to secure the services of a capable engineer to head the undertaking. It was the prac-

Erecting Shop, Bow Works, June 1898, almost preternaturally clean. Photograph National Railway Museum.

The Carriage Shops at Bow in June 1898. Photograph National Railway Museum.

tice to have a Locomotive Superintendent and during its lifetime, the NLR would appoint three men to the position. They were:

William Adams   1853 - 1873
John C. Park   1873 - 1893
Henry J. Pryce   1893 - 1908

The first, William Adams, remained with the company until he moved to the Great Eastern at Stratford in 1873. Adams was an engineering apprentice at the London works of marine engineers Miller & Ravenhill and later worked overseas in the same field. He was then involved with civil engineering projects – chiefly the installation of hydraulic equipment at Cardiff Docks, and also similar equipment in the NLR docks at Poplar. He joined the NLR itself in 1853 to look after locomotives. After his spell with the GER, Adams joined the LSWR in 1878, and embarked upon the work for which he is much better known.

Adams was succeeded by J.C. Park. Park began his railway career in Manchester and after a spell in Canada went to Dublin, to the Inchicore works of the Great Southern & Western Railway of Ireland. Several of his colleagues from this time would follow Park to Bow. Park had also worked for the LNWR. He designed the well known North London 0-6-0 goods tanks, principally for work around the docks. One of these is today the only remaining example of a Bow-built NLR locomotive. BR No.58850 was preserved by the Bluebell Railway on withdrawal in 1960. Park retired in 1893.

Henry Pryce joined in 1878; like Park

he had also started his railway career at Inchicore, and took responsibility for the Signalling & Telegraph Departments, also located at Bow. On Park's retirement in 1893 he also took control of the rest of the works, including the locomotive and rolling stock side. When the LNWR agreed to take over NLR operations from 1st February 1909, Pryce was one of the NLR officers who took retirement, at the end of 1908.

Establishing Bow Works

It was reported to the Meeting of Proprietors on 4th August 1854, that *'sheds and workshops, in which it is expected the repairs of engines and carriages will be carried out are being erected at Bow, as the most central and convenient spot. They are nearly completed, and as soon as they are opened, and the additional stock and locomotives provided, the whole of the working operations of this company will be carried out independently'*. These last were underlined in the record, to make the point! The accounts for the year up to 31st December 1854 show the cost of building the workshops at Bow as £31,505 13/- 2d. Twelve months later they show further expenditure of £10,169 3/- 11d.

There seems to have been little distinction at first between running shed and workshops. The separation of these two distinct operations, each with their own requirements, did not come about until later, when workshops were expanded to cater for ever increasing workloads and the locomotives used for day to day traffic were removed to separate running sheds.

At Bow, the original facilities were located in the 'V' of the Fenchurch Street and Poplar lines, with an entrance off Bow Road. These remained in use until 1882, when the running shed was moved to Devons Road and the original site used for the works extension (see section on Devons Road later in this chapter).

Despite extensive research, the exact opening date of the shops at Bow has not been ascertained. We do know, however, that the site was in use by October 1855, for a complaint was heard by the Board at its meeting held on 30th October 1855. It came from a Mrs Ram, who declared that 'her tenants from the estate were complaining about the noise from the company's workshops at Bow'. This is the first mention of Bow Works in the official Board minutes of either the E&WIDBJR or NLR Board meetings. The minutes for 28th October 1856 refer to a report received on tenders for a new steam hammer and tools for Bow Works, at a cost of £320; the NLR record for 18th August 1857 mentions a tender of £133, submitted for painting 'sheds at Bow'.

At a meeting held on 10th November 1857 the Board authorised payment of £400 to compensate Mr Gordon for land adjoining 'the company workshops at Bow'. At the following meeting, held on 24th November, it was reported that Mr Gordon was prepared to accept £420 and the payment was authorised. At the same meeting, the Board invited tenders for additional engine equipment at Bow, estimated at £230 by the Locomotive Superintendent William Adams. The tender price of £236 13/- from Hack & Son was accepted at the Board meeting on 5th January 1858.

Disastrous Fire

On 27th August 1858 a serious fire destroyed the carriage shed along with its contents, which included several coaches. The cause was the naked flame of a handlamp coming into contact with a container of varnish. The NLR Board received an initial report of the accident at its meeting on 31st August 1858. At the following meeting, on 14th September, a more detailed account was given and the Secretary reported, somewhat ruefully, that the accident 'should not have happened'. The building had been insured for £2,000 and the contents for a further £2,000. The same minutes record that the insurance on the locomotive shed should be increased to £10,000! The Board recommended that the settlement offered by the insurers should be accepted and that plans should be drawn up to increase accommodation, and alterations to the plans be made.

The carpenters employed in the carriage shed lost their tools in the fire. At that time, it was the responsibility of workmen to provide their own tools and to replace them as required. The tools lost were valued at £156 2/- 9d and the Board sanctioned the Locomotive Superintendent to assist NLR employees by financing up to half the cost of replacement.

At the Board meeting held on 28th September 1858, it was reported that the sum of £3,985 had been received from the Imperial Fire Office, which was only some £15 less than the insured amount.

In October 1858 proposals arose for the rebuilding of Bow carriage sheds; the Stores Committee reported to the Board that *'rebuilding of the carriage sheds should be undertaken on land recently acquired from Mr Gordon. Access to be obtained by bridging under the land which now separates the proposed site from that of the former premises'*. Cost of rebuilding was estimated at £5,000 and included a new carriage repair shed, a new forge and new paintshops (separated from the carpenters premises!). The plans allowed for the work to be undertaken in stages; there was an option for the carriage repair shed to be built initially for an estimated cost of £2,250, for instance, though this was not pursued.

The minutes also record that the engine shed was not big enough to accommodate all the company's locomotives and some were having to be housed 'in the temporary shed built by the Northumberland & Durham Coal Company'. It was also noted that the coal and ballast trucks were being repaired at Poplar, away from Bow. Poplar had at that time a smithy, lathes and stationary engines. The minutes conclude that the new carriage repair shed at Bow would allow for the Poplar buildings 'to be broken up' and

that tenders should be invited 'forthwith'. The lowest tender was received from Stephenson & Co. in October 1858, for £5,395, and this was accepted. Hack & Son submitted the second lowest at £5,479, which was to prove important, as events unfolded.

The Engineer reported on 23rd November that the schedule of work submitted by Stephenson & Co. was not acceptable to him. The Board resolved to grant the contract to Hack & Son, provided they undertook the work for the price submitted by Stephenson (£5,395). Hack & Son soon completed the task, the Board recording on 21st May 1861 that the firm had requested settlement of the account 'for erecting sheds and extensions to the repair shops at Bow'.

Further Expansion or a Move to Old Ford?

Additional land was soon required at Bow and by February 1862 the purchase of 17 perches (or an exchange for a parcel of NLR land) belonging to 'the poor of Bishopsgate' was under discussion. The Board resolved to exchange land if possible – if required to purchase, it would pay up to £100 for it. This was to result in difficult and lengthy correspondence with Mr Clapham, Clerk to the Trustees of St. Botolph, Bishopsgate. The Board heard on 4th November that Mr Clapham had valued the land at £700, a price the Board agreed to match if it was valued at that

Woodworking saws and other belt driven machinery at Bow in 1896. Building the compact little NLR coaches, hardly bigger than up-market horse boxes, was predominantly a woodworking exercise and as with other works processes (on all railways) the company did everything short of growing the trees. Raw timber and iron/steel castings and forgings came in to be fashioned by hand and machine into the vehicles the NLR needed. Photograph National Railway Museum.

by a 'mutually agreed surveyor'. The minutes for 16th December 1862 report that the figure should not exceed £900, while by 27th December the figure had risen to £800. By 13th January 1863 the Board had had enough and declined to purchase the land on grounds of excessive cost; it resolved instead to investigate the price of land at Old Ford, with a view to 'ultimate removal of the shops'. The Stores Committee was summoned to a special meeting on 20th January to look at property at Old Ford. Soon Mr Clapham was objecting to selling the whole of his plot, though he was prepared to sell the piece of land required to strengthen the company's boundary, for £100. This too fell through but Christ's Hospital in the meantime accepted an NLR offer of £310 per acre for land at Old Ford. By the spring of 1863, the matter was drawing to a close – the Old Ford land was valued at £2,009 and its purchase was agreed.

While the land wrangles went on, the Board sanctioned the purchase of a 20cwt steam hammer from Glenn & Rop of Glasgow, at a cost of £300. According to the minutes, the previous hammer had been installed in 1855 (though earlier minutes of 28th October 1856 throw doubt on the date) and was 'no longer capable of the work asked of it'. Additional tools were sanctioned on 5th May 1863, when it was reported that shaping machines and two bolt lathes should be purchased from Messrs. Shepherd Hill, for use in the workshops at Bow.

Plans for the new carriage sheds at Old Ford were submitted to the Board on 8th September 1863. These included a new roof for the existing sheds at Bow and a tender of £1,594 was accepted on 1st October. The work at Old Ford was delayed because of problems with an adjacent roadway; its purchase (at £188) was agreed but after that no more is heard of the proposed move to Old Ford.

Work was afterwards concentrated at Bow, and the site would eventually grow to cover 31 acres – accommodating locomotive, carriage, wagon, signal, telegraph, permanent way and advertising departments. The works was now self-sufficient, able to deal with most of the company's requirements, with a large erecting shop, foundry, smithy and machine shop. The NLR locomotives and most of its coaches and goods rolling stock were produced at Bow after 1863.

Further Expansion

On 15th December 1863 the Board agreed to purchase 7½ acres of land at Devons Road from Mr Ratford, at a cost of £1,000 per acre. Despite heavy investments in Bow, the NLR had continued to look for improvements and on 17th May 1864, plans were submitted for an additional carriage shed there. Mr Francis Hedges' tender of £4,144 was accepted on 28th June. At the same time, Adams requested enlargement of the existing boiler shops, estimating the cost of the work at £300. It was resolved to put it in hand. A shed for storing loco coal, at a cost of £250, was sanctioned on 20th July 1865. Further expenditure was agreed on 18th January 1866, for 'the Long Shed' to be fitted with ashpits, at a cost of £350.

On 17th May 1866 Adams reported on provisional arrangements with the Durham & Northumberland Coal Company, for the purchase of remaining coal stocks in store at Bow. The NLR also agreed to purchase further land occupied by that firm's coke ovens, at a cost of £2,000. So the works continued to expand, and later in 1866 various further arrangements were discussed; plans for the workshops were drawn up, 'following amendments made by Mr Ramsbottom' and additional land was to be bought, 'from Mr Ratford at Bow to provide any future extensions to the workshops'.

Additional equipment was also sanctioned by the Board and on 18th January 1866 it agreed to purchase a new planing machine and double bolt lathe from Messrs. Fairburn. A screw cutting lathe, brass finish shaping machine and a nut and bolt turning lathe were also agreed upon, to be supplied by Sheppard Hill.

The Locomotive, Stores and Traffic Committee

The Public Records Office at Kew has separate minute books for this committee from 1871 onwards. Prior to this, the decisions taken or recommendations made were incorporated within the main minute books. On 28th November 1871 it was reported that the working hours at Bow Works had been reduced to 54 hours per week (including 6 am until 1 pm on Saturdays). On 3rd December 1872 it was recommended that *'hot water heating apparatus be furnished to the new carriage shed at Bow, the painting and varnishing of carriages, rendering it necessary for the building to be properly heated'*. A reduction in the number of Foremen, from 12 to 10, was sanctioned on 4th November 1873.

On 2nd December 1873 it was decided to purchase a new boring machine to replace the previous one, at a cost of £115.

'Workmen's cab', used to ferry men between the works buildings at Bow.

Three compartment 1st Class coach No.99 at Bow, 1906. Photograph National Railway Museum.

Despite the minutes recording that it was worn out, it was decided to offer it for sale! The meeting of 3rd February 1874 heard of a fatal accident to locomotive fitter William Garbutt, killed by a light engine while crossing the line at Bow. The company had agreed to pay £10 compensation and the funeral expenses. Safety was obviously a matter of concern and the committee asked Mr Park to arrange for fencing to be placed around the doorway to the fitters' shop and to investigate the possibility of building a footbridge between there and the stationary engine shops.

Labour Saving Equipment

Much of the work of the Locomotive, Stores and Traffic Committee was involved in the everyday running of the railway. Hidden amongst the booking clerks' losses, employees' accidents, retirements, dismissals and other routine issues, was the sanctioning of improvements to the premises at Bow. Over the next few years the Committee would be heavily involved in the purchase of what the minutes call 'labour saving machinery'. In May 1875 it was recommended that a new steam hammer be purchased, in connection with 'making break (that is, 'brake') work' from Messrs. Thwaites & Carbutt, at a cost of £110. In June 1875 Park requested a cylinder planing machine, which was purchased from Craven Brothers at a cost of £410, and it was also agreed to purchase four lathes at a cost of £320 from the same source, 'to

replace those worn out'. Two new cranes were authorised in August 1875, for use in the running shed and wagon works respectively, at a cost of £100 and expenditure on 'labour saving machinery' continued with the purchase of a drilling machine from Cravens at a cost of £180. At the meeting of 1st February 1876 the Committee heard that the Company *'needed to expedite the completion of additional locomotives, in time for the Summer traffic requirements'.*

Additional Sidings

On 4th April 1876 additional sidings were authorised at Bow, to accommodate the Tilbury line service, thus avoiding the need to shunt trains on the main line.

Theft

There are several instances of employees stealing from the company. In 1876 for instance a Driver had been prosecuted for stealing timber from Bow Works and had received two months imprisonment. The harsh penalties, not to mention dismissal from the company, were obviously recorded to deter others!

Separating Works and Shed

As early as October 1876, the NLR was looking at problems deriving from the locomotive running shed being part of the works. On 31st October, Park explained that complaints regarding smoke and noise had been received and that the company might be compelled to move the engine shed to a new site. Park had obvi-

ously made some investigations and had identified a site owned by the Ratford Trustees at a cost of £12,000, which was ideally suited for the purpose. The NLR required only part of the site, but it would appear that the Trustees had decided on an 'all or nothing' sale. Park explained that should it be purchased, the land not required could be converted into a road and laid out for building purposes. The committee asked for the matter to be passed to the main Board for urgent consideration, with the recommendation that the entire property be purchased. Although it would take several years to come about, the land would eventually serve for the new Devons Road engine shed and associated housing alongside for the workers, in Devas Street, Empson Street and Marner Street.

Additional Workshop Space

On 10th October 1876 it was resolved to erect a new pattern and carpenters' shop. The purchase of suitable 'labour saving machinery', including a log saw frame, was approved at the same time.

Contract Work

At the meeting of the Locomotive, Stores and Traffic Committee held on 28th November 1876 it was reported that the company had secured a temporary contract for washing the LNWR carriages used on its Metropolitan services between Broad Street and Mansion House. Work was to be carried out at Bow, providing the NLR with an income of £13 a week.

More Machinery and Equipment

On 10th January 1877 it was agreed to purchase a new crane and traverser for the running shed. Bearing in mind earlier discussions on the separation of the shed from the works, it is clear that progress was not as quick as anticipated. Later that month (30th January 1877) £400 was authorised for a gas holder and associated equipment at Devons Road, allowing gas to be piped to the trains (for lighting) at a considerable saving. There were difficulties in washing out locomotive boilers due to poor water pressure and a suitable pump, from Messrs. Shand & Mason, was authorised at a cost of £150. Further 'labour saving machinery' was authorised on 3rd July 1877 for the saw mill, carriage and pattern shops, at a cost of £485.

In December 1877 difficulties were being experienced with the transport of carriage wheels from Devons Road to Bow Works. It was recommended that a tyre turning machine be transferred from the works to Devons Road and that a small 4 horsepower machine be purchased for £102 10/-, to drive it. A new wheel lathe was authorised on the 4th June 1878, from Messrs. Craven at a cost of £350. Another wheel lathe was authorised from the same firm on 5th August 1879, at a cost of £460; on 6th April the following year £780 was authorised for a new frame plate slotting machine (so that engine frames could be machined at Bow, avoiding outside contractors). On 3rd August 1880 a 35ft. turntable was agreed, from Cowans, Sheldon at £255. A further £220 was agreed for the cost of the turntable well and associated track

laying. A new wood planing machine was sanctioned on 31st January 1882, at a cost of £120 and a new screw cutting lathe for £150; on 10th October 1882 an automatic wood machine, band saw and drilling machines were approved at £193.

Works and Shed – Conflict Continues

On 8th October 1878 the Locomotive, Stores and Traffic Committee was reminded of the earlier conflict between the requirements of the workshops and the engine shed. There was difficulty with the amount of space available for stabling locomotives and preparing them, pending the provision of new facilities at Devons Road. The installation of two additional pits in the 'Long Shed', it was considered, would solve the problem – at least for the moment. The cost was £1,150. Later, on 3rd December 1878, progress on the pits was reported; the problem, it seems, had not been fully resolved, for the meeting authorised the construction of an additional shed, complete with pit, at a cost of £500, which increased capacity by a further seven locomotives. The cost of signalling alterations, to allow locomotives access to the proposed new lines at Devons Road, had been estimated at a cost of £110.

Reorganisation Planned at Bow Works

A meeting of 7th January 1879 examined plans for the reorganisation of Bow. It was suggested that the works be fenced off from the running line and that an overbridge be provided with a new central entrance, off Back Road. The plans included extending the foundry, a 75ft.

chimney for the wheel shop and a new furnace. The estimated cost was £4,523 but a decision was deferred until the Committee could visit the site and look at the suggestions themselves. The members must have been convinced for at the next meeting, held at Bow on 4th February 1879, the Committee ordered that the work be carried out, as an 'important and reliable addition to the premises'.

On 1st April 1879 Park reported difficulty in accommodating the increased number of trains at Devons Road and recommended the installation of six additional sidings; the Committee, ever alert to questions of economy, agreed only to three, at £100 each.

Problems at Bow

On 10th January 1882 Park submitted plans for a major rebuilding programme, which included the removal of the existing roof and a portion of wall. To accommodate the girders and columns for a 30 ton travelling crane, it was necessary to rebuild the wall higher, by eight feet. The new roof would include skylights. Costs were estimated at £9,000 but approval was deferred until the Committee, once again, could inspect the matter on the spot. This it duly did, a few weeks later and after careful examination, agreed the work was needed 'at once'. The matter was passed to the main Board for a decision. At the same meeting it was agreed to install a large illuminated clock in the works, complete with gas fittings. A tender for £49 from Messrs. Thwaites and Read was accepted.

Works grey 0-6-0T No.111 at Bow shed (later called Devons Road and surviving as such, to become BR's 'first all-diesel depot' in the late 1950s). Photograph National Railway Museum.

Second class compartment coach No.114. The plate has a date of 1905 and the legend 'Bow Road Works London E'. Photograph National Railway Museum.

More Sidings and Covered Accommodation

Further expenditure of £130 was agreed on 1st February 1881, for additional sidings at Bow. The following month a further four carriage sidings and sixteen short sidings for wheel storage were approved at Devons Road, at a cost of £725.

By November 1881 the drainage and paving for the new Devons Road carriage shed had been completed. The gas fitters shop, it was recommended, should be removed to the outside of the carriage shed at Devons Road, in order to avoid fire risk.

Chimney Trouble

Early in 1883 the company got notice from the Metropolitan Board of Works, concerning the unsafe condition of the chimney shaft at Bow Works. The offending chimney was reduced by 30ft. as a result

Overcrowding leads to new Engine Shed

By the spring of 1883 the erecting shops were either full of locomotives being repaired or new ones being built, and it could no longer serve as a running shed. Urgent approval was sought for the erection of two new running sheds and the necessary retaining wall, adjoining the Lea Cut. The work, it was stressed, should be completed by winter and it was authorised immediately, at a cost of £32,500. The need to separate the works and running shed had first been dis-

cussed back in 1876, but the time had now come when there was little option but to proceed!

On 29th May it was suggested that levelling of the ground and building the retaining wall and foundations for the two engine sheds could be carried out by a contractor while the 'superstructures' – the walls and roof, presumably – could be put up by the Locomotive Department. The Committee agreed to invite tenders for the work. Costings had been received by 3rd July 1883, and a local contractor, Bangs & Co., appointed for the work. By the end of the month (31st July), an order had been placed with the Dowlais Iron Company for the supply of some 120 tons of steel rail. In October, it was agreed to purchase blue Staffordshire bricks, mainly for paving, from Messrs. Hanley Brothers – it was also reported that the Lea Conservancy Board had agreed for the NLR to extract up to 80,000 gallons of water a day from the Lea Cut, providing it returned 40, 000 of them!

Work obviously took longer than the original plans estimated because it was 7th October 1884 before the new sheds were discussed further. At that meeting, it was agreed to provide the required machinery for the shed and to remove and relocate the turntable from the works to its new home. On 2nd December, it was recommended that a new 42 lever signal box be provided to allow movements to and from 'the new steam sheds'. This was approved at a cost of £300.

New Sheds Completed

Previous sources have identified the opening of the new sheds as 1882. The minute books, however, clearly show that the actual opening dates were rather later than has previously been recorded. The Committee meeting of 3rd February 1885 reveals the true story. Work on the two sheds had been completed 'with the exception of some internal fittings'. No.1 shed had been occupied since 1st November 1884 and half of No.2 had been in use since 20th December. The other half of No.2 shed would be occupied on completion of the necessary track works, which were still outstanding. Work had commenced on the water softening plant and a large underground reservoir had been commissioned. Minor works to the chimney shaft, furnace and lavatory block were still outstanding.

The estimate for the new steam sheds had been exceeded by £1,070 and a further expenditure of £2,500 was authorised for minor works. Problems were also being experienced with the river wall, which had to be strengthened and a large section renewed following collapse. With construction complete, the separation of works and running shed had finally been achieved. It would allow for the works to become better organised to achieve the objectives set in the following years. The further story of the 'steam sheds' (LNWR terminology, by the way) continues in the section: Devons Road (Bow).

Later Extensions to the Works

The Locomotive, Stores & Traffic Committee approved new accommodation, to adjoin the general stores. In order to provide the necessary space, several temporary buildings (used to store cast iron, permanent way materials, oil, spare equipment, bricklaying and boilermaking materials) were removed from the yard. The cost, which included extension of the Boiler (No.10) Shop, was estimated at £2,250 – for a building of 10,164sq.ft. When finished, it was 12,144sq.ft. Correspondence was still being exchanged between Mr Pryce and the Board regarding the actual and estimated costs, and the reasons behind it in 1902! At its peak, Bow Works employed some 750 staff.

Collision at Devons Road

Twenty-eight passengers and six staff were injured when the 9.30 am from Poplar to Broad Street collided with an empty coal train outside Devons Road signal box on 12th March 1900. Locomotive No.46, which was hauling the passenger train, sustained considerable damage to its front end.

Bow under LNWR Control

When the LNWR took over the day to day operations of the NLR in 1909, much of the activity at Bow Works ceased. A few of the staff were offered alternative posts at either Crewe or Wolverton, but the services of the others were 'dispensed with'. Bow was considered for total closure at one time, but managed to hold on with locomotives, rolling stock and road vehicles sent for repair from the LNW to utilise the spare capacity. Works Manager at this time was Mr Cox.

LMS takes over at Bow

After the Grouping in 1923, the newly formed London, Midland & Scottish Railway (LMS) found itself with two works in close proximity, for the LT&SR had established its own premises at Plaistow in 1881. The first LMSR Chief Mechanical Engineer was George Hughes, the holder of a similar post on the Lancashire & Yorkshire Railway (L&YR) which was one of the many companies that made up the newly formed entity. He despatched Henry Fowler, formerly of the Midland Railway, to London's East End to report on the situation. Fowler recommended that Plaistow should close, which was carried out in the autumn of 1925, with staff and equipment transferring to Bow. Stanley Whitelegg, formerly Locomotive Superintendent of the LT&SR (a position formerly held by his father Thomas and brother Robert) took over at Bow. He remained there until 1928, when he transferred to Horwich, being succeeded in turn by T. Lovatt Williams. By now, some of the old tank locomotives used on NLR services were beginning to show their age and some LTS 4-4-2Ts were supplementing them. By 1929, the LMS 3F 'Jinty' 0-6-0Ts had taken over all passenger workings and a great deal of the goods shunting work too. On 12th March 1932 the LMS closed the former MR repair shops at Kentish Town. The locomotive work was transferred to Bow, with Kentish Town retained for road vehicle repairs.

Nationalisation, Run-down, Closure

The 1947 Railways Act nationalised the main British railway companies to form British Railways, the new concern coming into being on 1st January 1948. Ini-tially there was little change, Bow continuing to operate much the same as it did under LMS ownership. Nonetheless, change was coming. The British Transport Commission (BTC) published an internal document *The Modernisation and Re-equipment of British Railways* in October 1954. This passed to the Minister of Transport in December and became public in January 1955. It is often referred to as 'The 1955 Modernisation Plan', although this is an unofficial title. The document covered the replacement of the then mainly steam locomotive fleet with more efficient diesel and electric traction. Like many such schemes, introduction was gradual – indeed steam locomotives were still being built as late as 1960 – but by 1968 all had been withdrawn from British Railways operations, save for three narrow gauge examples at work on the Aberystwyth - Devils Bridge narrow gauge line.

With implementation of the plan going on apace, it was necessary to look at the future of the many heavy engineering establishments then overhauling locomotives and stock. This review was carried out under the Chairmanship of Mr Mitchell. The inevitable decision to close Bow Works came as no great surprise at the time. So far as can be ascertained, closure took place in December 1959 by which time Bow employed 150 men. The last Works Manager, Bruce Carmichael, was a descendant of the Carmichaels who built the first locomotives for the Dundee & Newtyle Railway.

It is known that the works was running down in October 1959, when the *Railway Observer* reported 0-6-0s 44571 and 43989 in the erecting shops minus wheels and 0-6-0Ts 47455, 47483 and 47554 in

Loco coal wagon, No.12, built at Bow in 1894. Photograph National Railway Museum.

0-6-0T No.17, built at Bow in 1889. Photograph National Railway Museum.

the yard in ex-works condition. This was the last known recording in the railway press of locomotives passing through the works. The closure itself, remarkably, passed unreported in the railway press, and was not remarked upon even in the *East London Advertiser*, the local newspaper. From closure Bow Works stood empty, with a handful of staff employed for security purposes. In July 1966, the Greater London Council announced that the site would be redeveloped to enable 270 flats to be built in three five storey blocks. By early November 1966, demolition work was in full swing. Demolition of the 100ft. works chimney was witnessed by a cameraman from the *East London Advertiser*, whose four pictures of its downfall, appeared in the issue dated 17th November 1966. It was the end of a long and distinguished history.

Devons Road (Bow)
Earlier in this chapter, the lengthy process of separating running shed and works was outlined. The company completed its new steam sheds on land it already owned off Devons Road and these became (by a long measure) the principal running sheds for the NLR, the only other shed being at South Acton (see Chapter 2). The new Devons Road sheds stood close to the LT&SR Bromley-by-Bow station. The design and layout of the two buildings, backing on to the 'Limehouse Cut', owed much to the LNWR. No.1 had ten roads and served mainly for locomotives awaiting their next turn of duty. The adjacent No.2 shed was used for maintenance and servicing. A substantial 110,000 gallon

water tank stood behind the shed, with the area underneath put to good use, to accommodate the stores. A larger free standing water softening plant was installed around 1903; a similar plant was also installed at Broad Street.

After the NLR passenger operations were taken over by the LNWR in 1909, the shed principally provided for NLR freight work and for the non-electrified passenger services. In 1916 electrification of most services led to a reduction in passenger work and with it the closure of the little shed at South Acton. The LNWR did not allocate a code to Devons Road, for technically it remained NLR property. At the Grouping in 1923, however, it got the code W11 as part of the LMS Western Division, until it was grouped with the former LTS sheds, along with the Midland Division sheds, in July/August 1934. At the time of transfer Devons Road had an allocation of 73 locomotives. Following reorganisation in January 1935, a separate LTS Division was created under the principal 'concentration' shed, Plaistow. New codes (carried on the smoke box doors) were:

13A	Plaistow
13B	Devons Road
13C	Tilbury
13D	Shoeburyness
13E	Upminster

No.1 shed was reroofed in the 1930s in standard LMSR concrete and glass style. Space was less of a problem by then and No.2 shed was demolished in 1935; a new concrete coaling plant was built at the same time. Following Nationalisation further reorganisation took place in early

1949. By now there was little non-electrified passenger work left, most of the steam services having fallen victim to wartime closures (see Chapter 11).

The ex-LTS sheds passed naturally to the London Midland Region of BR but soon, in January 1950, they were transferred to the Eastern Region; Devons Road, however, still linked in its workings to the old LNW, remained part of the LMR's Western Division. The 1949 reorganisation resulted in the following shed codes being adopted from January 1950:

1A	Willesden
1B	Camden
1C	Watford
1D	Devons Road (Bow)
1E	Bletchley

'Britains first all-diesel depot'
BR's Modernisation Plan resulted in the move away from steam to diesel and electric traction, and the gradual phasing out of steam locomotives. Each BR Region was allowed to adopt its own policy and the LMR chose Devons Road for its experimental conversion exercise. In 1957, the depot had an allocation of 41 steam locomotives, most of them LMS 3F 'Jinty' 0-6-0Ts. Conversion for diesel working began in September that year, Inside No.1 shed, five tracks were retained for stabling purposes, while the space occupied by the other five roads was divided off to form a three road maintenance 'facility'. Removal of the old smoke troughs from the roof meant that improved lighting could be installed. The space between the tracks allowed high level inspection tracks to be built and between the run-

Ten ton goods brake van, No.18 built in 1898. Photograph National Railway Museum.

ning rails, new inspection pits were provided with built-in lighting, to aid inspection. The maintenance area was also fitted with gas heating and the facilities were a great improvement on the cold and dark of latter day steam operation.

Conversion work was complete on 25th August 1958, when the last steam loco-motives left the depot. By 1959, Devons Road had just over thirty Type 1 main line diesels and eight 0-4-0 shunters. Despite this, it continued to provide coal and water for visiting steam locomotives from other depots, working in and out of the docks.

Closure

The LMR gained much valuable experience from the Devons Road programme but 'being the first' did not make its future secure. Depots and workings were further rationalised, the dock traffic disappeared and 'Britain's first all diesel depot' closed on 10th February 1964, its

Engines under repair in Bow Works on 16 April 1955. These include 3F 0-6-0T No.47487, 4-4-2Ts Nos. 41921 and 41941, and 3F 0-6-0s Nos.43729 and 43762. It maintained a 'Midland' air to the end, losing its LNWR connections when it was incorporated into the Midland-owned LTS Section by the LMS. Photograph Brian Morrison.

Bow Works, impossibly cramped by later standards, in LMS days. The usual 'customers' are in for repair, 3F tanks, 'Tilbury' tanks and 0-6-0s. Photograph Rev. Arthur Mace, Milepost 92½.

locomotives split between Stratford and Willesden. Some books have referred to Devons Road being transferred to the Eastern Region shortly before closure. Bearing in mind its geographical location, this would have made sense, but exhaustive checks with staff who worked in the motive power organisations of both Regions, have failed to confirm this. Staff, including Senior Management, are adamant that Devons Road remained a LMR depot right until demise and was never part of the ER. The adjacent sidings were used for the storage of redundant steam locomotives after closure and the shed building stood empty for many years before the site was redeveloped.

Bow Today
There is little now to suggest any of the bustling activity once carried out at Bow, for most of the site is now an industrial estate. The former main line to Poplar now forms part of the Docklands Light Railway (DLR) Stratford-Poplar section, and the area is served by Devons Road station (see Chapter 15). The former Devons Road shed site was at one time considered for the DLR depot, but this was ultimately built at Poplar.

'The usual suspects' at Bow in the LMS period. Bow really operated as an 'outstation' or subsidiary works and was convenient for smaller engines based in or near London, particularly the local tanks which did not travel well. That did not preclude the occasional 'exotic' visitor when other works were overloaded. Fitters based in London, at sheds such as Cricklewood, could do their six months 'works' experience here instead of Derby, avoiding the need to lodge in digs away from home. Photograph Rev. Arthur Mace, Milepost 92½.

If dereliction set in on the NLR as a kind of general malaise, then it was, if anything, worse in the east. This is Stratford Low Level, looking south to North Woolwich with Southern Junction Box mistily in the distance. Thoroughly GE territory rather than NLR, but the line came into the 'North London' fold in 1979.

In the gloom under the main station at Stratford Low Level.

Chapter Six
Eastern Expansion

Eastern Counties Railway (Stratford to Victoria Park)

The line from Stratford to Victoria Park, often referred to as the Victoria Park branch, was opened by the ECR on 15th August 1854. It was, however, left to the NLR to operate a passenger service to and from Stratford Bridge. This was achieved by attaching and detaching coaches from through trains from Hampstead Road to Fenchurch Street at the junction at Victoria Park. A locomotive then worked trains forward to Stratford Bridge. In the reverse direction the locomotive was detached after shunting the coaches on to the west bound service. No station was provided at the junction at first. Victoria Park was a popular destination at the time, particularly on Sundays, when folk would walk in the park to enjoy the fresh air and country atmosphere.

A station, consisting of two Spartan platforms, was under construction at the time of the ending of the Crimean War. To mark the peace, a large celebration was held in Victoria Park, on 29th May 1856. So that visitors could reach the event, the station was specially opened on the day. At its official opening to passenger traffic, later in the year on 14th June, the station was still lacking canopies and waiting rooms, which only appeared later. It was known as 'Victoria Park, Hackney Wick' for a time and was advertised by that name in timetables of the period. Around 1859, it became known simply as Victoria Park. The junction was used for goods traffic from 1st January 1855, mainly at first wagons from East Anglia, for onward transfer to other companies.

A new four platform station opened at Victoria Park on 1st March 1866, east of the former site. The platform serving the Down Stratford line was used only for placing coaches detached from Up Poplar line trains. No footbridge or subway was provided and this platform could only be reached by crossing the tracks. The detaching of through coaches was discontinued shortly after opening and this platform was no longer used – it was eventually demolished in the 1890s. Trains then operated as a Stratford Bridge-Victoria Park shuttle, arriving and departing from the same platform. This gave cross-platform interchange with Poplar-bound trains and a change of platform for westbound passengers.

Completion of the new station allowed the operating companies to take stock of the service. From 1st September 1866 NLR trains were diverted into the main line station at Stratford before continuing to Barking via the Lea Valley line, a service which lasted only a matter of weeks. The Stratford Bridge-Victoria Park shuttle was taken over by the GER on 1st November 1866. This arrangement only lasted until the following year, when the NLR once again took control of the shuttle, for a year, with the GER assuming responsibility for the following year. This 'alternate year' arrangement continued until 1874, the final NLR train leaving Victoria Park for Stratford Bridge on 31st October 1874. The line came fully under GER control from that date and would not rejoin the 'NLR' network for 105 years! (see Chapter 15). A new footbridge was provided at Victoria Park in 1891, linking the three remaining platforms. A second entrance, complete with its own booking office, opened in 1899 and was referred to locally as the Hackney Wick entrance. The GER extended the service beyond Stratford Bridge to Canning Town on 1st October 1895.

LINES TO NORTH WOOLWICH
(this section of line is included here, though it only officially joined the latter-day 'North London Line' in 1979)

1. The Eastern Counties & Thames Valley Junction Railway

In 1844, George Parker Bidder proposed building a line from Stratford (ECR) to Bow Creek, where the River Lea meets the River Thames, an ideal site for a wharf – Thames Wharf. Opened in 1846, the Eastern Counties & Thames Junction Railway ran for 2¼ miles and was operated by the Eastern Counties Railway from the start. Once the line towards North Woolwich was opened, this section was included in the North Woolwich line.

2. The North Woolwich Railway

In 1847, the line from Stratford to Thames Wharf (Canning Town) was extended to a point on the River Thames opposite Woolwich. Woolwich, on the south bank of the river, had been served by a ferry from the north shore since ancient times. The newly constructed railway terminus was duly named North Woolwich and the railway operated its own ferry service, its attention firmly focused on the Royal Arsenal traffic. At the time the railway was constructed, the area around the new station consisted of only a few houses and a pub. The station building was rebuilt in 1854. That same year, the ECR began a service from North Woolwich to Fenchurch Street via Stratford.

Up until the opening of North Woolwich the line had been freight only. To cater for the new passenger business, stations were opened at Stratford Bridge (later Stratford Market) and Barking Road (later Canning Town). Thames Wharf continued to be a major destination for goods traffic.

A branch from Canning Town served East India Docks and also the Pepper Warehouses on Bow Creek, which had been in business long before the coming of the railway. (The branch only opened in 1848, after the ECR took out a lease on the warehouses.)

Stratford Low Level opened in 1854 with Custom House station following a year later. It was well located to serve the original Victoria Dock. From Custom House, branches were built to both Gallions and Beckton. Tidal Basin station opened in 1858. In the previous year, an iron works was opened at Canning Town, leading to the rapid development of the area.

The building of railways south of the River Thames led to a decline in traffic destined for Woolwich itself. To compensate for this, the ECR built the Royal

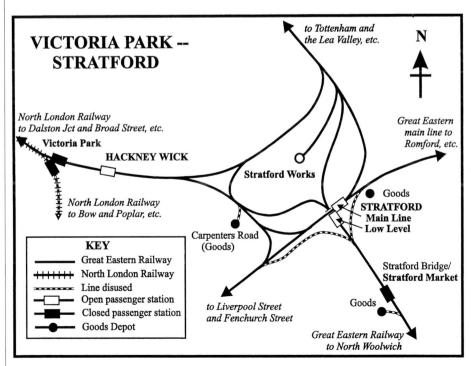

VICTORIA PARK -- STRATFORD

to Tottenham and the Lea Valley, etc.

N

North London Railway
to Dalston Jct and Broad Street, etc.

Victoria Park

HACKNEY WICK

North London Railway
to Bow and Poplar, etc.

Stratford Works

Great Eastern main line to Romford, etc.

Goods

STRATFORD
Main Line
Low Level

Carpenters Road
(Goods)

Stratford Bridge/
Stratford Market

KEY
- ——— Great Eastern Railway
- +++++ North London Railway
- ------- Line disused
- —▭— Open passenger station
- —■— Closed passenger station
- —●— Goods Depot

to Liverpool Street and Fenchurch Street

Goods

Great Eastern Railway to North Woolwich

Postcard view of Victoria Park station (the GE joined the NLR just to the east). A most imposing building it was too.

Pavilion Gardens (now the Royal Victoria Gardens) opposite the station, to drum up some tourist traffic at weekends and Bank Holidays. The industrialisation of the area and the development of what had become the Royal group of docks soon followed, laid out on what had lately been open marshland. Bidder, the promoter of the original railway to Canning Town, had been actively buying up land before forming the Victoria Dock

Company in 1850. The Royal Victoria Dock opened five years later; as a result the railway now crossed the entrance lock on a swing bridge and the dock company agreed to divert the ECR line. In exchange, the dock company took the original ECR formation for its own use, and this became known as the Silvertown Tramway.

There was a yard at Silvertown for exchanging traffic with the tramway,

which linked the various factories and industrial premises, all of them served by a multitude of sidings. The line ran parallel with Silvertown Way from Victoria Dock to the main freight yard at North Woolwich. The lack of roads before the 1930s and the numerous level crossings was good for revenue, as virtually everything in and out of the area went by rail.

Abbey Mills spur opened from the LT&SR at West Ham, initially to freight (31st March 1858) and to passengers on 1st June of the same year; it gave direct access from North Woolwich to Fenchurch Street, without having to travel via Stratford.

The Great Eastern
In 1862 the ECR, along with other railway companies, formed the Great Eastern Railway (GER). In 1874 Liverpool Street station opened alongside the NLR terminus at Broad Street. The GER's previous Bishopsgate terminus was relegated to goods use.

Development of Silvertown
The opening of the station at Silvertown in 1863 is an interesting tale in its own right. Samuel Winkworth Silver was born in 1791 and despite his name became one of the pioneers of the rubber industry. In 1852, he bought up a marsh and built there the India Rubber, Gutta Percha and Telegraph Cable Works, later the Silvertown Rubber Company. In order to make his factory more accessible, Silver persuaded the GER to open a station

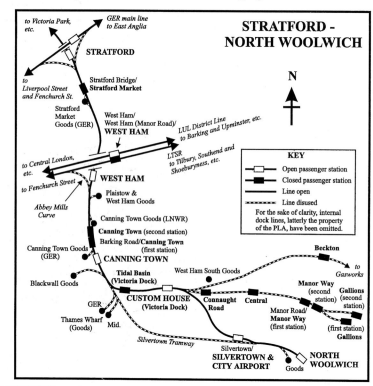

nearby. On opening it was known locally as Silver's Halt and the neighbourhood became known as Silver's Town. Over the years the name has been amended to become Silvertown.

Expansion of the Docks

The London & St Katherines Dock Company became the owners of the Royal Victoria Dock in 1864. Such was the increase in trade that an additional dock soon became necessary. Opened in 1880, the new dock (the Royal Albert) was connected with the Royal Victoria at one end and with the Thames itself at the other, at Gallions Reach. Once again, the main line found itself crossing the channel between the docks on a swing bridge and the dock company agreed to yet another diversion, this time by building the Connaught Tunnels (often referred to today as Silvertown tunnel) underneath the waterway, whilst again taking over the original formation for itself. Part of the agreement allowed the GER to use the former formation for any trains too heavy for the gradients in and out of the tunnels.

Stratford Market

The GER purchased sixteen acres of land adjacent to Stratford Bridge station for the building of large warehouses; eight, each 60 yards long by 50 yards wide, opened on 1st October 1869, built by W. Bangs & Co. of Bow. Trains arrived via Stratford or Fork Junction – thus avoiding Stratford Low Level station. The section south of Stratford had four tracks, two devoted to passenger trains. Access

to the Market required trains to back into the sidings, two for each warehouse. The warehouses were well designed, each having good access and covered loading/unloading arrangements for the horse drawn carts. Unloading direct from railway wagons was both easy and swift. Twelve sidings could accommodate over 400 wagons and four roadways allowed up to 200 carts to be dealt with at the same time. Much of the produce came from East Anglia and each merchant had his own office inside the warehouses. The GER granted the traders permission to sell produce on, or direct to customers at the site, thus creating, in effect a market – hence 'Stratford Market'. While the GER charged rent for the warehouse space, the real benefits were from the traffic generated.

Taking fruit and veg by rail ceased before closure of the market itself, and the sidings continued to see some works trains, particularly during the GER voltage conversion from 6.35kV to 25kV in 1976/77 and, later, on the former LTS lines in the 1980s. Works trains used in electrifying the route from Dalston Western Junction to North Woolwich (1983-85) also worked out of Stratford Market sidings. There was also postal traffic during the Christmas period. After several years of inactivity, the site was cleared in 1994 to allow construction of the new Jubilee Line maintenance depot.

Stratford Bridge station had been renamed Stratford Market on 1st November 1880. It was rebuilt in 1892 to the north of the former station and renamed Stratford Market (West Ham) in 1898.

The GER opened its own printing works opposite Stratford Market station in 1893. It was extended in 1901 and at its peak employed some 260 staff. It was responsible for the output of GER tickets, advertising, publicity and information material, including timetables. Finally closing in 1951, the building remains in use today for light industry.

Barking Road station was rebuilt in 1873 on its original site and renamed Canning Town. A new station was built in 1888, on the north side of the Barking Road bridge – the two earlier structures had been on the south side.

A service was introduced on 1st January 1880, from Palace Gates to North Woolwich to carry labourers from the Wood Green and Tottenham areas to their work in the docks.

Ferry Monopoly Ends

The monopoly of the GER ferry service from North Woolwich came to an end in 1890, when the London County Council began operating its own free ferries in direct competition. To rub salt into the wound, local authorities in both East and West Ham (which had previously relied solely on the railway for its transport needs) began operating trams in the area.

In 1923, the GER became part of the newly formed London & North Eastern Railway (LNER), created as a result of the 1921 Railways Act. The LNER undertook considerable work on Bow Creek (Canning Town) from 1928 until its completion in 1935. Dredging and deepening took place and during the same period new retaining walls were built.

Spiritual needs as well as the requirements of the docks were met at Silvertown; this is St Mark's Church and Vicarage, the Silvertown Tramway (the 'Woolwich Abandoned Line') in the foreground with the line to Custom House running off to the right. Note how open the land is at this early time.

The 1930s and Beyond

Canning Town station was rebuilt by the LNER in 1932 and on its completion was the fourth station to serve the area. The formation of London Passenger Transport Board in 1933 soon affected the North Woolwich branch. LT initiated the replacement of trams with trolley buses and by 1937 they had reached North Woolwich, with passenger figures on the branch falling dramatically. Roads, too, were being improved. Prior to 1934 they had been difficult to negotiate, thanks mainly to the many level crossings which were often shut against road traffic to allow lengthy shunting operations to take place on the complex internal dock lines. This changed with the opening of Silvertown Way and the Silvertown bypass, both in 1934. Again there was a considerable decline in both freight and passenger revenue.

The Second World War was to have a devastating effect on the North Woolwich branch. On the night of 7th September 1940 it suffered extensive bombing and the station building at North Woolwich received a direct hit, losing the roof and the upper floor as a consequence. The platform canopies were also badly damaged and several trains stored in the station and adjacent sidings were destroyed. Later in the same year, Tidal Basin station between Canning Town and Custom House were heavily bombed and finally closed to passengers in 1943. The line was under constant threat and there was a continual need to patch up and repair tracks and stations; all around, the bomber's trails of destruction were changing the area beyond recognition.

Decline

Decline was inevitable after hostilities ceased and North Woolwich finally lost its through services to Fenchurch Street following the closure of the Abbey Mills curve on 27th July 1958. It was retained as a siding, accessible from the upper junction only, until final closure in August 1960. North Woolwich still had its remarkable service across London to Palace Gates but this too was withdrawn in 1963, leaving a local shuttle service to and from Stratford Low Level. Stratford Market station closed in 1957 and freight services were withdrawn from North Woolwich in 1970. A signing on point remained at Canning Town until around 1972 with an establishment of just two drivers. There had been eight in the 1950s, when there was still traffic from the docks.

Despite these losses, the North Woolwich-Stratford diesel multiple unit continued to shuttle back and forth. It would not be long before it would receive the attention of the transport planners of the Greater London Council (GLC) and become part of the North London Line – NLL (see Chapter 15 for the continuation of the story).

CONNECTING LINES
1. The Beckton Branch

In 1868, the 'Gas, Light & Coke Company' began work on a large gas works at a place now known as Beckton, on the marshes to the north of Gallions Reach. Work was complete in 1870 and to house the workers, a small town grew up round about, taking its name from the Governor of the company, Simon Adams Beck.

The gas works had its own coal dock for unloading the ships from the Northumberland and Durham coalfield. In 1871, the company built its own railway from Beckton to Custom House, a mile and 60 chains in length. Most of the incoming coal was taken off at two piers jutting out into the river. Pier No.1 was equipped with fourteen 30cwt cranes, while No.2 pier had twelve 50cwt cranes. Once the wagons were loaded, they proceeded on high level tracks to the weigh bridges, before continuing to the unloading point, where the coal was discharged through an opening in the floor of each wagon. The branch gained little from this traffic but it did, however, deal exclusively with the works' waste material, coke, tar and spent lime.

A small station was built at Beckton, mainly for the gas workers, with services coinciding with shift changeovers. The platform was just sufficient to accommodate the short four wheel coaches and the structure was little more than a works halt. The GER took over operation of the Beckton line in 1874, and trains afterwards began their journeys at Stratford Low Level, with ticket checking taking place during the Custom House stop. Passenger operations were withdrawn in 1940.

The internal railway system at Beckton was eventually to comprise some 41 miles of track, over thirty locomotives and more than 1,300 wagons. It was not unknown for twenty or more trains to be in traffic at any one time on the system. The system had three engine sheds including a roundhouse with ten roads and its own workshops which employed some 600 men, looking after the locomotives

Silvertown station, probably about 1950, looking towards Stratford. The Silvertown Tramway goes off to the left. It was a dreary district, poorly-built with crowded houses squeezed in between any number of factories and workshops. Everything, of course, was much knocked about by German bombs.

North Woolwich terminus in LNER days with, beyond, the elegant station building fronting the river.

and rolling stock, stationary boilers and other specialist equipment. Beckton employed some 4,000 men at its peak and could produce four million cubic feet of coal gas an hour.

After the war, Beckton was one of the areas chosen for 'prefabs' to rehouse East Enders, who had lost their homes during the war. Despite this influx of residents, the railway remained closed to all but goods traffic. The last train ran to Beckton on 1st June 1970, though the line did not officially close until February 1971. Wilting before North Sea natural gas, Beckton Works too closed that year, although it had not taken coal deliveries since 1969.

The Parliamentary Bill for the extension of the Docklands Light Railway to Beckton was first lodged in 1986, with construction work commencing in June 1989. This line is built almost on the former formation from Custom House to Gallions (see next section) as far as Cyprus station, although the trackbed and almost everything else had long been removed, along with sections of the former Beckton works internal system. Much of the new line has been built between the dual carriageways of Strait Road, with stations located beneath roundabouts. The DLR Beckton branch opened in March 1994.

2. The Gallions Branch
The dock company had an extensive railway system linking docks and warehouses and the building of a passenger only branch from Custom House to Gallions Reach was a logical move. Keen to promote Gallions Reach for deep sea passenger ships, the company built a hotel adjoining the station, for travellers arriving and departing from passenger ships. Amongst the passenger liners to use Gallions Reach were those of the Peninsular & Oriental Steam Navigation Company.

The Gallions branch opened to traffic on 3rd August 1880 with intermediate stations at Connaught Road, Central and Manor Road (the latter rebuilt in 1926). A bay platform was provided at Custom House for the Gallions branch trains, the dock company's own trains operating the shuttle to and from the Gallions terminus. The GER took over the operation of the line in 1896, but ownership remained with the dock company.

The bombing of East London was to affect the branch greatly of course. On the night of 7th September 1940, the same night as North Woolwich station was hit, the line was extensively damaged and the passenger service ceased as a result. Freight traffic had dwindled in the 1950s and it was used for wagon storage. Final closure took place on 17th April 1966 though the line had not been used for some years.

3. The Internal Docks Railways
It is hard to visualise it today, but until fairly recent times, London Docks were the busiest in the world. Today the Royal Docks have been stripped of all their commercial activity, and shipping in and out of the Port of London is concentrated on the deeper stretches of the Thames at Tilbury. Now the docks are being transformed from urban wasteland and are enjoying regeneration into thriving residential and commercial areas. The docks were the very hub around which the East End was developed and the dockers' homes and communities grew up round about. All relied on the railway for contact with the outside world and transport of the very freight they were loading and unloading in and out of ships. The docks themselves were divided into three groups; East and West India (Blackwall), Millwall and The Royals. Each was connected by a comprehensive railway system which came under Port of London Authority ownership in 1909. Access to the Blackwall and The Royals was from the North Woolwich line.

Blackwall
Blackwall Docks were divided between two sites, at Blackwall and Canning Town, only the latter being reached from the North Woolwich line (the docks at Blackwall are covered in Chapter 1). Located at Bow Creek at the mouth of the River Lea, Canning Town was larger than Blackwall Dock and could handle up to eight barges loading simultaneously. Transfer between the railway system and the internal railway network was through Thames Wharf yard.

The Royal Docks
The Royal Dockyards consisted of the Royal Victoria, Royal Albert and King

George V Docks. Covering over 600 acres, of which one third was water, the internal railway comprised some seventy miles of track. Unlike the other docks, The Royals also dealt with passenger liners, with portable accommodation for passengers and customs being moved around the various berths between departures and arrivals. The docks were the busiest on the north side of the Thames.

Connection between the Royal Docks' own railway system and the GER was made via the Victoria Exchange Sidings. These were made up of some thirty-one roads, with a capacity for 1,200 wagons. The building of the King George V Dock in 1921 saw further development of the Port of London railway system and new opportunities for interchange traffic.

Top and above. Custom House station, another half ruin amid a field of wartime destruction and damage. The North Woolwich line was diverted through Custom House on construction of the new Royal Victoria Dock.

The Great Eastern's North Woolwich terminus about 1910, showing the busy goods yard. The water tower and coal stage constituted an 'outstation', one of the many outposts of the Stratford empire, with a 'fitter in charge'.

Beckton station, built for the workers at the giant gas works which sprawled all around. No one would expect it to be any sort of architectural jewel...

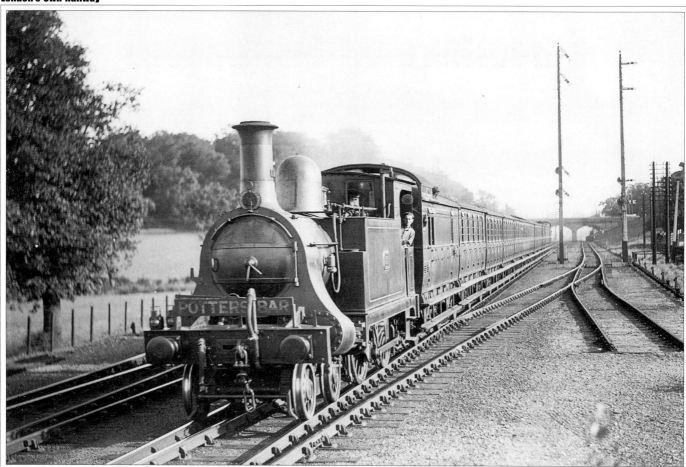

The NLR 4-4-0Ts on the Great Northern contrived to look ancient (especially with their geriatric sets) even as the 1920s wore on, especially against some of the bigger Gresley types. they were of 'an earlier century' to a degree more profound than almost any other type working fast(ish) trains on a main line in England by 1914, let alone 1930. Here is one on a Potters Bar train, on the down main at Greenwood box south of Hadley Wood south tunnel. The line on the right is the down slow (goods); this is the point where the four tracks reduced to two, a two mile bottleneck until 1959.

7491 (the four figure numbers came in after 1934) in the north London suburbs with an LMS set. Photograph Collection R.C. Riley.

Chapter Seven
Great Northern Connections

The NLR and the Great Northern Railway

Although Great Northern goods traffic had been carried by the NLR since early days, it was not until the 1870s that passenger services were introduced. The GNR was not enjoying the best of relationships with its customers in the early 1870s. At that time, its line into Kings Cross consisted merely of single Up and Down lines, approaching the terminus through a series of tunnels. Kings Cross opened on 14th October 1852, although an earlier terminus and its large goods yard, just to the north of the current and north of Gasworks Tunnel, had opened on 12th December 1850. The GNR built up a considerable suburban business in addition to its extensive goods traffic and express passenger trains and to ease congestion at the terminus, new suburban platforms were opened in December 1874. A connection was opened to passengers on 17th February 1868, from Kings Cross to the 'Widened Lines', which allowed the GNR to serve Moorgate Street.

In 1872 the GNR gained Parliamentary approval for construction of a new line, little over a mile in length, from Finsbury Park to the North London Railway at Canonbury. This was intended to carry both goods and passenger traffic, though the latter was dependent on the GNR obtaining approval from both the NLR and the LNWR to run services into Broad Street. The line opened for goods traffic on 14th December 1874 and gave the GNR access to the docks at Poplar (where it built its own warehouses) and to a goods depot at Royal Mint Street, near to the Tower of London. This had been acquired from the London & Blackwall in 1861. The GNR also opened a goods and coal depot at Hackney Wick, on 1st March 1878.

Commuting Crisis

By January 1875 commuters into Kings Cross were becoming frustrated, to put it mildly. Services were held up frequently on the approaches to Kings Cross, often behind coal trains awaiting entry to the many goods yards on the approaches to London. A 'crisis' meeting was held that month at the *Great Northern Hotel* adjacent to Kings Cross station. This was chaired by Samuel Waddy, a Queen's Council Barrister and MP, who later became a well known judge. As a result, pressure was put on the GNR to sort out its problems and to pursue the use of the recently opened Finsbury Park-Canonbury line, to gain access to Broad Street for some of its services, and to relieve the congestion at Kings Cross. The GNR immediately opened negotiations with both the NLR and its bigger partner, the LNWR. Whilst the NLR was keen to reach agreement, the LNW was against the idea and refused permission. To get its agreement, a compromise had to be worked out which allowed the NLR to operate trains to and from Broad Street and GNR stations, using NLR locomotives and rolling stock.

A trial service began on 18th January 1875, with twelve Up and Down trains – six on the main line to Barnet (now New Barnet) and six on the branch to High Barnet. The experiment was successful and regular services began running on 1st February 1875, with timetables and notices of the period describing it as the 'opening of the Finsbury Park-Canonbury line to passenger traffic'. The new official timetable of 1st February saw the services increased in both directions to Barnet (from six to nine trains), High Barnet (six to sixteen trains) and to Enfield (now Enfield Chase) for the first time (nine trains in each direction). These trains had quick turnarounds before working back to Broad Street.

Additional Trains

May 1875 saw the service further developed with nine trains serving Alexandra Palace, recovering from a major fire of two years before to become an important leisure attraction. A limited Sunday service began operating to Wood Green, Alexandra Palace on 5th June 1875. The NLR began running trains to Hatfield on 1st August 1877 but the service was short-lived and was withdrawn on 30th November of the same year. Another attempt was made to serve Hatfield during May and June 1879. At that time, the seventeen or so miles may have proved too much for the NLR 4-4-0Ts and the four wheel coaches then in use, having to put in fast timings to avoid delaying GNR express trains over this

16581 with one of those heroically long NLR sets on the GN main line. Photograph Collection R.C. Riley.

16566 at Wood Green with an LMS set – nowhere else were the 3F tanks used on lengthy and heavy suburban trains. Nothing seems to have been recorded concerning the work involved but it could not have been a sinecure by any means. Photograph Collection R.C. Riley.

heavily used main line. The service ran briefly again between July and October 1883.

Potters Bar got through services from 1st July 1880 – initially just one train a day – leaving Broad Street at 4.25pm and returning from Potters Bar at 5.45pm. A second train was added in 1881, a third in 1886 and by 1888 the number had increased to four. That year 62 trains served the GNR corridor. These worked in both directions and included:
Enfield (19 trains)
High Barnet (18)

New Barnet (7)
Finsbury Park (6)
Alexandra Palace (5)
Potters Bar (4)
East Finchley (2)
Wood Green (1)
The number of trains rose to 63 in each direction in 1905 and reached a peak of 65 the following year.

Tight Timings
Timings on the GN trains were extremely tight bearing in mind that they were made up of four wheel coaches hauled by

ageing 4-4-0 tank locomotives. For example, the 5.56pm from Broad Street was given just eleven minutes to reach Finsbury Park, including a stop at Dalston Junction. Once out on the main line, timings were even tighter. The 7.01pm train from Broad Street was given just nine minutes to cover the section from Finsbury Park to East Finchley.

Canonbury Tunnel Accident
A serious accident occurred on the Finsbury Park-Canonbury line around 9am on the morning of 10th December

In the 1880s there were more than sixty weekday trains booked out of Broad Street to GN destinations, including the branches, such as High Barnet, Enfield and Alexandra Palace. By 1929 these stood at forty, beginning at 6.05am and finishing at 8.12pm with a mid-day gap from 10.29am to 3.35pm and this remained the basis of the service pattern until 1939 and the outbreak of war. 7482 waits to leave High Barnet on 5 June 1937. Photograph H.C. Casserley.

In March 1938 a small batch of Stanier 2-6-2Ts, Nos.79, 82, 105 and 155 from distant parts such as Alsager and Llandudno Junction, went to Devons Road Bow for the work; No.79 with its new 13B shed plate was on a GN service shortly after that time. Photograph Collection R.C. Riley.

1881. The locomotive of an Up train burst a boiler tube at Dalston, coming to a halt and blocking the line. Due to an error in interpreting the different bell codes then in operation on the different companies' lines, trains continued to run towards Canonbury from Finsbury Park. As a result of four trains entering Canonbury Tunnel in close sequence, *three* collisions occurred, killing four passengers and a Guard. The Board of Trade report into the accident led to the Railway Clearing House developing a standard set of bell codes for use on all lines, thus avoiding the confusion that had caused this accident.

Below. Jinty 7517 bursts into the light at Highgate (on the High Barnet branch) with the 4.40pm from Broad Street, 5 June 1937. The whole of the NLR/GN Broad Street service was suspended on 11 September 1939 in the desperate days of that year but a few trains were started again on 4 December. Bomb damage forced the suspension of these in turn from 4 October 1940 and after the war, from 30 July 1945, such trains as were run again used LNER engines and stock. Photograph H.C. Casserley

The NLR 4-4-0Ts did more than half a century on the Great Northern suburban work, though thought was given to their replacement almost immediately after Grouping. The LMS tried an ex-LNW 0-6-2T, No.1009 and a Fowler 2-6-2T was also tried but, oddly, it was the 3F 'Jinty' tanks which replaced the NLR old timers in the early 1930s. This is 16599, near Greenwood on the GN lines with a characteristic NLR set, during that period. Photograph Collection R.C. Riley.

Timeless gloom at Broad Street.

Chapter Eight
Under Threat

Bus and Tram Competition

The threat from omnibus companies was first drawn to the attention of the NLR Directors in the 1870s. While there was some minor loss of revenue to the horse drawn buses on local traffic, the continuing rise in other traffic far outweighed this. The rapid increase in omnibuses could not be under-estimated however; such rivals, together with the tram and later trolleybuses, would affect the flows of all inner suburban operators.

The introduction of electric trams in North London from April 1901 and their rapid development thereafter, was to cause much concern. Trams had first appeared in parts of London in 1861 but had been less than successful. They reappeared in 1870 and by the 1890s had expanded to some 130 route miles; the steam operated NLR was no match for the trams, which were cheaper, faster and had more stops, and NLR traffic fell dramatically. Labour disputes, wage demands and the increasing cost of coal caused the Directors to look for economies. In addition to competition on the surface, electric underground railways were also developing, eating further into NLR receipts.

At its peak, around 1900, the NLR was carrying some 45,000,000 passengers and 3,200,000 tons of freight annually. Between 1900 and 1905, however, the number of passengers using Broad Street fell by 4%, representing a decline of some 13% in net revenue. Ironically, the competition was to play a major part in regeneration of the North London Line in the 1980s (see Chapter 15). Integration with other transport forms is now seen as an opportunity; at the turn of the last century it was considered a threat! There was only one course of action available and the NLR Directors considered electrification, in 1899, 1904 and 1908, but were unable to implement a scheme.

The LNWR Takes Over

In order to keep costs down, the NLR Directors agreed in 1908 that the company's day to day operations be taken over by the LNWR, from 1st February 1909. Despite this, the NLR continued to remain an independent company until 1922, when the LNWR took it over completely. The majority of the NLR's senior management retired at the end of 1908. George Newton Ford, the last NLR Traffic Superintendent, transferred to the LNWR at Euston where, in 1911, he became responsible for the Southern Division, between Euston and Stafford. The NLR became little more than a Division of the LNWR, which vastly improved the financial situation and increased productivity.

Under new management, instructions were issued to staff banning the use of LNWR bogie rolling stock on trains to NLR stations such as Richmond or on through workings to GNR or LTSR stations. A further batch of four wheel coaches was built at Wolverton in 1910 by the LNWR, for use on NLR services.

All railways ran on paper and tea, and that remained true from NLR days through the LNWR and LMS to BR in the 1960s. This is the office at South Acton in July 1965 – that stool may well have come into the world at the same time as the 4-4-0Ts...

Caledonian Road & Barnsbury in 1960 with electric set (later class 501) travelling east. The building with the rather generous ventilation is the gents' toilet block.

A short branch line (part of the LUL District Line) provided a shuttle service between Acton Town and South Acton until closure on 1 March 1959. Prior to this trains operated between Hounslow and South Acton from electrification on 13 June 1905 until 14 February 1932. The shuttle service came into operation from that date and was operated by single car electric units. Photograph R.M. Casserley.

Chapter Nine
Electrification Plans

Great Northern
The neighbouring Great Northern, over which NLR trains operated (see Chapter 7) was also under tremendous pressure from overcrowding and was unable to satisfy the demand for its services. In 1903, it commissioned Dick, Kerr & Company to report on electrifying its system. The report assumed that the GNR Directors would be able to persuade the NLR to electrify the line from Canonbury Junction to Broad Street, then used by NLR trains bound for GNR destinations. The short length of line (1 mile 20 chains) from Canonbury East Junction to Finsbury Park was earmarked for electrification under the consultant's proposals. Despite the study, the plan did not proceed and locomotive-hauled operations continued until the 1960s.

London & North Western
The initial proposals date back to the early days of the century when the LNWR was desperate to provide two additional tracks from Watford to Euston (making six altogether) which became known as the 'new line', a term still in use today by many railway staff! This initial proposal included an underground section from Kilburn to Euston, with a loop serving platforms under Euston station. In 1911, however, the LNWR Directors sanctioned the electrification of most of their London suburban system, which of course now

included the NLR. The original scheme was adjusted in favour of electrifying the slow lines into Euston itself and making greater use of the newly acquired terminus at Broad Street, and also building a junction with the London Electric Railway (LER) at Queens Park, then under construction – thus splitting the traffic three ways!

The system employed was 630v DC 3rd/4th rail, electrical contact being made via an outside 3rd rail and returning via an insulated centre 4th rail. Although 4th rail is no longer used by main line operating companies, the system is still standard on London's Underground and can be found on Railtrack lines where joint operation currently takes place (from Kensal Green to Harrow & Wealdstone and Gunnersbury to Richmond, for instance).

The first electrified section opened on 1st May 1914, from Willesden Junction to Earls Court via Addison Road (now Kensington Olympia). The section from Kensington Olympia to Earls Court now operates as part of London Underground's District Line.

Power Supply
In 1913 the LNWR began building a coal-fired power station at Stonebridge Park, adjacent to the Euston-Watford 'new line', to supply electricity, though power for the Gunnersbury-Richmond section came

from the LSWR. First World War restrictions delayed the construction and it did not open until 1916. The station was initially capable of producing some 20,000KW, though after the end of the war in 1918, it increased to 30,000KW, increasing again in 1933 to 46,000KW. Electric sub-stations were built at Acton, Broad Street, Camden Road, Dalston, Highbury, Willesden and West End Lane.

Coal was delivered in hopper wagons direct to the nearby sidings and then shunted onto coal staithes for unloading. The coal was then released into the chutes below, which were capable of holding up to eleven days' supply. Stonebridge Park could supply all the needs of the d.c. system and also the 'domestic' supply for both Euston and St. Pancras stations, surrounding offices (Euston House for instance), carriage sheds, goods depots and so on. Stonebridge Park closed on 30th July 1967; electricity was then taken from the National Grid, supervised from the Electric Control room at Willesden. Stonebridge Park prior to closure had been able to supply power to the National Grid!

Wartime Restrictions Slow Progress
Wartime shortages of labour and materials meant that progress on the other parts of the electrification scheme was slow and it was 1st October 1916 before electric trains began running from Broad

Single car District Line unit leaves the London Underground station at South Acton for Acton Town, 8 November 1958. The LT single platform station was alongside the main station at South Acton, on a higher level. Photograph H.C. Casserley.

Street to Richmond and Kew Bridge. At Broad Street only platforms 5-9 were electrified and only two of the four tracks from Broad Street to Camden Road (known as the 'No.2' lines). This remained the case until around 1937 when the bridge over the GNR was rebuilt. A new junction was installed at Barnsbury, the junction at York Road electrified and the section of the 'No.1' lines from Barnsbury to Camden Road electrified, using the 3rd/4th rail system. This allowed the electric service to continue while the 'No.2' line bridge was renewed. This section remained in use until around 1961, when the electrification on this stretch of the 'No.1' became disused.

The LNWR station at Chalk Farm was demolished as part of the electrification scheme, although the NLR platforms remained. This allowed the reorganisation of the track layout and the provision of two additional running lines burrowing underneath the main lines. To start with, a peak hours only Broad Street to Watford electric service started operation on 16th April 1917, over the former Hampstead Junction Railway (see Chapter 3) via Willesden.

Completion of the Electrification Scheme

The LNWR electrification was finally completed on 22nd July 1922, when trains began running between Euston and Watford Junction. A fifteen minute interval service began from Broad Street to Watford Junction. Full implementation of the scheme also saw the electrification of the Watford Junction to Rickmansworth line, and the addition of a new line from Watford Junction to Croxley Green. Further sub-stations were brought into use at Camden Bank, Queens Park, Stonebridge Park, Kenton, Headstone Lane and Bushey. The LNWR electrification, including the NLR, saw

the introduction of three types of trains. These are detailed below.

Siemens Stock

Built by the Metropolitan Carriage & Wagon Company of Birmingham, these units were delivered in 1914 and put into service on the Willesden Junction to Earls Court services from 27th November of that year. The electrical equipment was supplied by the Siemens Brothers Dynamo Works and throughout their working lives they were known as Siemens Stock. They were fitted with hand worked sliding doors.

They spent all of their time working either the Earls Court or Kew Bridge services from Willesden Junction High Level, and when the Earls Court services were withdrawn in 1940, they went into store. Three sets were refurbished mechanically in 1946 and used on rail cleaning and staff train duties. They were converted in 1951 to undertake AC overhead electric trials and eventually saw service between Lancaster (Castle), Lancaster (Green Ayre), Morecambe and Heysham. The fourth unit was similarly treated in 1957 and sent to the same line. They were withdrawn from BR service on 1st January 1966.

Siemens stock originally carried the LNWR purple-brown with white upper panels. From 1924, LMSR crimson lake livery was applied. This was carried until BR days when all units, returning from works, had unlined malachite green, which was itself replaced by a darker olive green in 1960.

Oerlikon Stock

The first batch was constructed for the introduction of the LNWR electrified services in 1916. Delivery commenced a year earlier and the units were stored at Croxley Green Depot pending the start of electric services in October 1916. Built

as thirty-eight three-car units, they were officially formed as nineteen six-car sets (running as three-car units off peak), with five spare motor cars to allow for their extra servicing requirements. The motor cars were built by the Metropolitan Carriage, Wagon & Finance Company (MCW&F), Saltley, Birmingham. The trailers and driving trailers came from the LNWR's Wolverton Works. Built to operate on the 630v d.c. 3rd/4th rail system, the electrical equipment was manufactured by Maschinenfabrik Oerlikon, near Zurich, Switzerland. As a result the units were known as Oerlikon Stock throughout their working lives.

Modifications were carried out to the luggage compartments from 1920 at Wolverton Works, and each had an additional window fitted to form a guard's compartment. Additional orders were placed in 1921 for a second batch of thirty three-car sets and three spare motor cars. As before, MCW&F built the motor cars and Wolverton Works the trailers. Most of the Oerlikon stock was replaced by the Class 501 units (known in pre-T.O.P.S. days as 57ft. stock) from 1957 onwards.

One three-car unit (M28269M - M29736M - M29036M) remained in service until 28th April 1960 on the Watford Junction to Croxley Green branch and another (M28249M - M29733M - M29033M) was used until October 1963 for shunting duties at Stonebridge Park. The motor car from this set has been preserved and is part of the collection of the National Railway Museum at York. It is the oldest 'EMU' in Britain. A further two-car set (M28262M - M29027M) was used by Dr H.I. Andrews for testing rail and wheel adhesion problems.

Vehicle No. M29776M was used in the early 1960s as a mess room for staff at Leighton Buzzard shed; other vehicles saw out their days at Ilford Car Sheds

An Oerlikon unit arrives at Richmond in 1953. The track to the right of the train (with the signal at the stop position) permitted through running from the North London to the old London & South Western line. The gas works and a timber merchants were both rail served.

and one survived as an Instruction Coach at Stonebridge Park.

Livery details are similar to the Siemens stock; they never received olive green, being withdrawn from 1957, but the Stonebridge Park shunter and the Dr. Andrews set did receive yellow warning panels on both cab fronts.

GEC Stock

The compartment stock was built in two batches in 1927 and 1932, to reduce over-crowding then being experienced on Broad Street services, particularly in peak hours. The situation was so bad that the Wembley Medical Officer regarded events as 'a nuisance to public health'. The House of Commons was informed of matters on 26th March 1926 and this resulted in the reappearance of some steam hauled workings on the Earls Court services. New trains were quickly authorised and these were known as GEC stock throughout their working lives, their electrical equipment coming from General Electric. A number of traction motors, however, were supplied by Metropolitan Vickers, and one motor coach had compatible Parkinson Crompton equipment, so it could run connected to Oerlikon stock. The GEC 1927 stock had one weak field position whilst the later 1932 stock had two; the Oerlikons by contrast had none. Metropolitan Cammell built the motor cars, Clayton the trailers and the Midland Railway Company, Birmingham the driving trailers. The later 1929 and 1932 vehicles were built at Wolverton.

Similar compartment stock was ordered for the Liverpool electrified services and also for the Manchester to Altrincham line. The London area stock was built to a slightly larger loading gauge, with higher roofs than the earlier stock, thus preventing its use between Addison Road and Earls Court. In 1939, coach No. 29401 was sent to work on the Manchester to Altrincham section.

Some damaged vehicles were withdrawn from use as early as 1941, but the majority continued working alongside Class 501 units delivered in 1957 (see Chapter 14). The GEC stock survived until 1962, when rationalisation of the fleet allowed withdrawal. One three-car unit was sent to Stonebridge Park to replace the three-car Oerlikon shunt set.

The units were delivered in LMSR crimson lake livery and subsequently appeared in BR malachite green and then olive green, as described for Siemens stock. Two units also carried the lined olive green livery.

Maintenance Depots
To maintain the trains,
a purpose-built running shed was completed in 1914 at Mitre Bridge, Willesden, adjacent to the LNWR main line. It was requisitioned as a Government store during the First World War, before opening for its intended purpose with the start of electric services from Euston to Watford on 10th July 1922. It closed on 13th September 1963, and the site is now a large scrap yard, clearly visible from Willesden Junction High Level station.

Electric traction required its own workshops and these were provided at Stonebridge Park. The depot and adjacent power station covered some seventeen acres and was able to undertake all electrical and mechanical work. Two roads, each fitted with a 25 ton overhead crane, served the repair shops. The works building included an Armature Gallery, where motor armatures could be repaired and rebuilt if required. Only in the event of major body repairs and repainting did the units need to visit Wolverton Works. Stonebridge Park also had an adjacent eight road running shed. The former works was turned over to wagon repairs and in more recent years it has been a heavy repair depot for InterCity coaches, although it is currently disused. The site closed for EMUs on 27th June 1966.

Although off the NLR, a further depot was opened as part of the 1911 electrification scheme – Croxley Green near Watford, on 16th April 1917. After closure of both Mitre Bridge and Stonebridge Park, this depot became responsible for all d.c. traction units on both the Euston to Watford and North London lines until it too closed, on 4th November 1985, when the last of the class 501 units was withdrawn. The replacement units from the Southern Region were never allocated to Croxley Green and it was demolished shortly after closure (see Chapter 15).

Broad Street Train Crew Depot
The introduction of the new electric services resulted in the transfer of crews from South Acton and Devons Road to Broad Street around 1916, and signing on facilities, along with a mess room, were set up for them. Staff trains continued to run from Bow, where the majority of Devons Road staff lived, to take the train crews to and from their units. These were steam worked, as Devons Road remained a steam shed right up to its brief moment of fame as 'Britain's first all diesel depot' (see Chapter 5).

Broad Street maintained a signing on point right up until closure of the station on 30th June 1986. Broad Street train crews were then dispersed to other depots in the London area, while train crew provision on the NLL passed to both Stonebridge Park and Watford depots.

Holding Sidings for Electric Units
Electric units not required outside the peak periods needed somewhere to stand, and coach holding sidings were electrified in the following locations:
Dalston Junction (adjacent to station)
4 sidings 6 cars each
Caledonian Road & Barnsbury
2 sidings 6 cars each
Kensal Green Junction
3 sidings 3 cars each,
2 sidings 6 cars each
Acton Central
2 sidings 6 cars each

From 1933 some of the units on the North London Line were stabled at Euston Up side shed. Others were stabled at Watford Junction station and the bay platforms at Willesden Junction Low Level station (new line).

Below. **Brondesbury in 1961, looking east. A three car Oerlikon unit calls at the platform with a train for Broad Street.**

No.22, its plate reading 'rebuilt Bow Works 1900'. It was a 'No.1 Standard' 4-4-0T, a large class designed by Adams and rebuilt by Park.

Horse vehicles on 'the Caley', outside Caledonian Road & Barnsbury station.

Chapter Ten
Battle Lines

The First World War (1914-1918)
The railways came under Government control in August 1914. The NLR assumed greater importance than ever before as troops, ammunition and supplies were moved to the docks, bound for Europe. At times the traffic flow was so great that the passenger service was suspended. Not all was freight, for over 7,000 troop trains travelled over the North London during the war.

Wartime Closures and Withdrawals
It was inevitable that some stations would be forced to close during the conflict and that some services would be withdrawn. The shuttle service from Bow to Plaistow was stopped in 1915. Chalk Farm station closed from 1st January 1917 to 10th July 1922, so that rebuilding of the junctions at Chalk Farm could take place. Maiden Lane also lost its services, on 1st January 1917 but unlike Chalk Farm, it never reopened. Another wartime measure saw the closure of linking arrangements between Hackney and Hackney Downs and from Bow (NLR) to Bow (GER), though only the latter proved permanent.

Bombs and Bomb Damage
Bombing was not confined to the Second World War (see Chapter 12), for London endured its first ever air raid on 31st May 1915. As a result, crowds flocked to Dalston Junction to seek shelter, overpowering company staff and police officers in the process. Following this action, substantial air raid shelters were built for use by the public, as well as staff, at several NLR locations, including Shoreditch goods yard (for over 1,000 people), Bow station (four arches), Broad Street station (cellar and arches) and Poplar (basement under warehouse). Other companies operating in north London also provided public shelters. The

GNR for example, had such facilities at Poplar Dock, East India Dock and Royal Mint Street. The NLR also provided staff shelters at various locations, the only proviso being that they were subject to approval by the company's own engineers.

The docks were the principal target for the enemy raiders but despite their attentions the loss of rolling stock was minimal. Of the 2,080 coaches and wagons in NLR service during the Great War, only twenty-one were destroyed by enemy action. The threat from the air resulted in 'black out' conditions during the hours of darkness. There were no blinds in the coaches, so to avoid detection by enemy airmen the NLR painted the windows dark blue.

Buildings were damaged and hundreds of panes of glass broken in a Zeppelin raid on Broad Street on 8th September 1915. Fortunately there were no human casualties, although several of the horses employed on shunting and delivery cart duties were killed.

Air raids caused considerable damage to the NLR. On 23rd September 1916, several bombs fell between Bow and South Bromley, including a hit on Devons Road depot, damaging several coaches beyond repair. On 1st October 1917 the running lines between Shoreditch and Haggerston were hit and Dunloe Street Signal Box damaged.

A Junction at Last
In 1916, a wartime junction between the Hampstead Junction and the Tottenham & Hampstead (T&H) line was installed at Gospel Oak. The junction remained in use until 1920 and was removed sometime after, leaving the independent T&H platform in use in its pre-war guise.

Suspension of Services
Several times during the war it was found necessary to suspend passenger services

to keep the line free for military traffic. Under peacetime conditions goods were not run during the 'peak' hours and all traffic was suspended on Sundays during the times when church services were held. During the war period, passenger services were often suspended throughout a whole weekend.

Wartime Requisitions
Unlike many of the railway companies, the NLR did not have any of its locomotives requisitioned by the War Department's Railway Operating Division for service overseas. A train of 27 coaches did go to France in 1917 for ambulance use, though this stock had been made redundant by the start of electrified services in 1916. A train of four wheel coaches later served as a 'Demob' train for troops returning home, and ran in conjunction with some Army wagons.

The Ultimate Sacrifice
Sixty-four NLR employees were killed whilst on active service in the forces. In remembrance, a memorial was erected at Broad Street station in 1921. After closure of Broad Street in 1985, the memorial was relocated and now stands by the station entrance in the car park at Richmond station.

The end of the North London Railway
Four years of conflict had imposed a considerable burden on the railways throughout Britain and by the end of the war there were major arrears in maintenance. In recognition of the railways' contribution to the war effort, the Government acknowledged the need for a major reorganisation. The 1921 Railways Act caused most railway companies to be placed into four large groups, and the NLR and its larger partner, the LNWR, were scheduled for merger with the Midland, Lancashire & Yorkshire, Highland, Caledonian and several other smaller companies to form the largest of the four groups, the London, Midland & Scottish Railway (LMS). With such radical changes on the horizon, the NLR Board agreed for the company to be taken over completely by the LNWR in July 1922.

Reorganisation takes effect
On 1st January 1923 the LNWR itself was no more, although being the largest and most powerful of the companies forming the LMS, it was to influence policy in the new organisation on everything apart from motive power, where Derby and the former MR ruled the roost, at least initially. The other companies with which the NLR was linked had been 'grouped' too of course, the GER and GNR becoming part of the LNER and the LSWR passing to the Southern.

The NLR War Memorial, erected in Broad Street station in 1921, and removed to Richmond in 1985.

Gospel Oak. The Second World War institutionalised neglect on the North London and its stations.

NLR 4-4-0T No.37, renumbered by the LMS 6466.

Chapter Eleven
Between the Wars

The New Railway Takes Shape
Whatever the drama and romance of the Grouping, the humble lines in North London carried on much as before. The LMS had 19,000 track miles and some 250,000 staff. In addition to its railway activities, it owned 25 docks, piers or harbours, 66 ships, 4,000 road vehicles, 8,000 horses, 28 hotels, 25,000 houses, aircraft and over 500 miles of canal. Other interests included heavy engineering in its own workshops, warehousing, removals, holiday homes, farming and gas supply! It was a truly massive undertaking, the largest private railway company ever to operate in the world.

Link up with the former LTSR
One of the first benefits was the relief of congestion on the former LTS lines from Fenchurch Street, which the LMS had inherited under the Grouping. It is likely that the LNWR and LTS were already working towards such integration following the passing of the 1921 Railways Act. The LMS was, therefore, in position to introduce through trains from Broad Street to destinations such as Southend, on 1st July 1923, which used the curve from Bow to Bromley as the link between the two systems. Through trains from Broad Street to Southend and other former LTSR destinations were withdrawn, however, in 1935.

Station renamings and closures
There were some station renamings as a result of the new organisation, with the LMS now owning two stations close to each other in some towns or city areas. Accordingly Kentish Town became Kentish Town West on 2nd June 1924, to differentiate it from the LMS station on the former MR main line, while Acton was renamed Acton Central on 1st January

1925. Mildmay Park station closed on 1st October 1934.

Rebuilding and Improvements
Some refurbishment took place at Shoreditch, a rebuilding of the booking office made necessary by the widening of Old Street and Kingsland Road between 1926 and 1929. The SR began rebuilding Richmond station in 1935 and was keen to amalgamate what had previously been two stations, old and new. Designed by the SR staff architect, J. Robb Scott, the new station was officially opened on 1st August 1937. It is one of his later designs, based on the famous 'Odeon' cinemas of the Art Deco period.

Operations 1928-1931
Retired signalman George Peacock still remembers vividly the operations during this period. He had joined the LMS in 1928 as a Porter/Signalman at Broad Street and his duties required him to work both the No.1 and No.2 boxes there. At the time he was taught NLR signalling practice but within a year these had been superseded. In 1929, George found himself working at Dalston Junction station, which was so busy between 7.30am and 11am that a Porter/Signalman was rostered to work the No.2 lines at Western Junction Box, so that the signalman could concentrate on the No.1 lines. During this period, the two men would undertake some 1,400 lever movements! Between 8am and 9.30am, the morning peak, no freight trains were allowed over the line.

Station Staff
During the 1920s the stations were extremely busy. To give some idea of the staff numbers involved, the situation at Dalston Junction was as follows:

1 Station Master
2 Foreman
6 Porters
3 Booking Clerks
3 Signalman (Station Box)
3 Signalman (Western Junction Box)
3 Signalman (Eastern Junction Box)
Staff were spread across three shifts, the Station Master sharing his duties with his two Foreman, giving seven members of staff on duty per shift.

The Forgotten Railway
Despite its successful operations elsewhere, during the 1930s the LMS was blamed (presaging much later events!) for running down services on the North London Line (NLL), making stations difficult to find, and being responsible for the low morale of the staff. Passengers complained about lack of signs from streets and drew attention to the superior signing provided by other companies like the SR. The NLR became known during this period as 'the forgotten railway'.

During this time the line received additional electric multiple units (see Chapter 9), six new rakes of bogie coaching stock to replace ancient four wheelers on the LNER (former GNR) services and some of the new LMS 3F 0-6-0Ts in place of vintage NLR locomotives. Some bridge reconstruction work to permit heavier locomotives was carried out (mainly over Camden Street and the three span high bridge over the LNER main line) as well as some signalling improvements.

Gunnersbury Changes
The fifth platform face at Gunnersbury was closed in 1930 and the Chiswick curve, linking the Metropolitan District Line and the Richmond line from the north, closed on 9th May 1932.

London Passenger Transport Board
In 1933, the London Passenger Transport Board (LPTB) was formed as a single company to look after the Underground and some sub-surface lines, such as the Metropolitan Railway. The previous year, the double track of the South Acton-Acton Town line (District Railway) had been singled, with the remaining track used by the single car shuttle service between the two stations.

War Again
The railways serving the area were about to enter yet another conflict, one which would bring about major closures and withdrawals. With preparations for war gathering apace, on 1st September 1939 the LMS passed into Government control, along with the GWR, LNER, SR and LPTB. The railway would emerge from the war vastly different from the one that entered it.

2648 (an LNWR plate) after the Great War, at Bow on 5 April 1924.

Above and below. Forget the blackout! Gospel Oak recalls the darkest days of the war, even five years after, in 1950. Similarly (lower) the roof did not survive hostilities. *Below right.* 'Bloodied but unbowed' would seem to sum up the state of Hampstead Heath station after the Second world War

Chapter Twelve
The Second World War 1939-45

War Footing
Despite what many may think, the railways were well prepared for the outbreak of war – which had seemed imminent back at the time of Munich. As early as 1937 for instance, LMS workshops had been engaged in tank design and the manufacture of aircraft parts. The company also undertook detailed planning (just in case) for troop movements, munitions and the quick dispersal of warehoused material away from the vulnerable docks, particularly the Port of London. The setting up of a strategic reserve of foodstuffs and other essential materials demanded extensive train operations to the north and Scotland, where threats of invasion were considered less serious.

By the end of August 1939 the company was very much on a war footing and the North London Line (NLL) as it was known, would play a vital role in the movement of both troops and freight. Its many connections with other lines were essential to the war effort and when general mobilisation of troops was ordered in the same month, it would see a rapid increase in the number of trains over its metals.

A Major Effort
By now every section of the LMS was actively involved in preparing for a Second World War. Workmen busied themselves building shelters while the Signal & Telegraph Department laid alternative communication systems, to enable the trains to continue running should damage occur. The necessary black-out arrangements had to be implemented and crews taught how to work trains under these trying circumstances.

During the weekend war was declared the 3,000 LMS headquarters staff at Euston House suddenly found themselves transferred to 'The Grove' at Watford, a large country mansion. This was accomplished with a minimum of fuss and disruption.

Evacuation
London was considered the prime target for enemy bombing, so the company drew up plans to enable it to evacuate large numbers of children aged 3-13 away from the capital in the shortest possible time. These plans were drawn up during the summer of 1938 and finalised in July 1939. When the demand came, the company needed just 24 hours notice to put the plan into action. 1,400 special trains were run over a four day period. Broad Street and the North London Line were integral parts of the evacuation. Even the electric units were utilised to convey evacuees to other stations, where they changed into waiting steam trains. The planning that went into this exercise was to serve the company well, for as the war developed, the children of large cities in the North West, Midlands and Scotland had to be treated in a similar way.

Evacuation was not just confined to children. During the period 31st August-4th September 1939, thirty-two special goods trains left the warehouses of various London docks conveying consignments of meat and butter. A few days later, seven trains were organised to carry chests of tea!

Freight
A prodigious goods traffic was generated during the six years of the war, with the LMS running over 90,000 additional trains. The NLL was used for major traffic flows between the various companies' lines and as defence changed to attack, to the docks for onward movement to the continent.

'Is your journey really necessary?'
All but essential travel was curtailed by early 1940, allowing the railways to concentrate on moving troops and equipment, while the *Luftwaffe* did its best to make this task difficult if not nearly impossible at times. Tremendous pressure had been put on the railways during Christmas 1939, with people travelling to spend Christmas at home, so the *'Is your journey really necessary?'* campaign was not unexpected. One early casualty of the wartime travel restrictions, which led to service withdrawals, was the line from Kew Bridge to South Acton. It closed to passengers on 12th September 1940 and the conductor rail was subsequently lifted, no doubt to be stored for emergency repairs elsewhere on the system. This line remained open for goods traffic and remains so today.

Wartime Measures
One wartime measure, from 6th October 1941, was the withdrawal of 1st Class accommodation on electric trains, all tickets becoming 3rd Class. The LNER withdrew trains from Stratford to Victoria Park on 1st November 1942; no longer an interchange, the rest of the station closed when the LMS withdrew its trains

on 8th November 1943. Trains from Broad Street to former GNR destinations were withdrawn from 4th October 1940. The junction at Gospel Oak, between the former T&H line and the NLL, installed initially for First World War traffic, was re-instated on 11th March 1940.

Bombing was intense during 1940. Haggerston closed after suffering heavy damage on 6th May 1940. Even after it closed the station was again heavily bombed, in October 1940, with the street level booking office severely damaged. Shoreditch was also closed from 3rd October, although a bus service was provided for a while and the booking office continued to issue tickets until the station shut officially on 17th November 1941. There was a constant need to patch up the damage to allow the trains to run, supplies for ships having priority over passengers. In September 1940 the London docks, along with the various goods depots around Poplar, endured substantial damage from heavy bombing.

All four tracks near Highbury & Islington suffered extensive bomb damage in March 1941. The high retaining wall and one of the overbridges collapsed and required major repairs. The lines themselves were soon reopened, although work continued for several weeks on the structures.

A flying bomb inflicted severe damage on the southern end of Poplar station in 1944. Services were cut back to Bow and the service from Broad Street to Poplar officially ceased on 14th May 1944. The booking offices remained open to sell tickets for the replacement buses, before finally closing their doors on 23rd April 1945. The buses stopped and the line was closed to passenger traffic for good, or so it was thought!

During the war a land mine destroyed a school adjacent to Gospel Oak station, inflicting in the process severe damage to the down platform buildings. It was repaired on a temporary basis until rebuilding took place in the 1950s.

LNW electric sets, to Broad Street (top) and Richmond (lower) at Acton Wells Junction, 4 May 1957. The venerable LNW sign reads NOTICE TO DRIVERS (how anyone could see it in anything but perfect visibility is a good question) SPEED NOT TO EXCEED 35 MILES AN HOUR THROUGH THE JUNC[NS]. Photographs R.C. Riley, The Transport Treasury.

Chapter Thirteen
A Period of Recovery

The period after the First World War had seen great changes; the effects of the 1939-45 conflict were even more profound. On 1st January 1948, the emerging BR was formed into six Regions, each of them (with the exception of the North Eastern and the Scottish) took control of the old company routes and territories. What had been the LMS (more or less – Scotland was 'detached') became the London Midland Region (LMR). Some boundary changes took place in 1951 and in the 1960s further changes saw the boundary between ER and LMR established at Dalston Lane bridge. Two stations were renamed on 25th September 1950 – Chalk Farm became Primrose Hill and Camden Town reverted to its 1853 title, Camden Road.

Closures and Withdrawals

The spur from Bow to Bromley saw its last Southend-bound excursions in 1955, and London Transport withdrew the shuttle service from Acton Town to South Acton on 28th February 1959.

Broad Street Alterations

In the early 1950s, the main station block at Broad Street was leased out for non-railway use. A new booking office was provided in 1957 and extra accommodation provided for station staff on the concourse. Extensive roof repairs were carried out in the 1950s, while further benefits included a new enquiry office, new toilets and the removal of gas lighting in favour of electric lights.

In 1968 the train shed was shortened because of its then appalling condition, so that it covered a much smaller area – really only the space nearest the buffer stops. The station stood silent for much of the time except for the trains which ran back and forth to Richmond and rush hour services to Watford Junction and former GNR destinations (Hertford North and Welwyn Garden City). Passenger numbers had fallen to a trickle, dereliction had set in and tracks were removed from platforms 1 to 4, and No.9.

Broad Street received another blow in 1976, when the GN electrification scheme resulted in the diversion of through trains from Hertford North and Welwyn Garden City. The line to nearby Moorgate was electrified with 25kV overhead line, as part of the scheme, thus allowing the ER trains to work into their own city terminus.

Station Rebuildings and Improvements

Several stations were rebuilt during the 1950s. The platform buildings at Hampstead Heath were reconstructed in 1953 (cost £42,000), although it had to wait until 1968 for a new booking office! Gospel Oak was rebuilt in 1955 (cost £45,000). Highbury & Islington a year later (cost £30,000) and Willesden Junction High Level followed in 1957 (cost £49,000). Some of these buildings replaced war damaged structures and all were built in the concrete and brick design of the period. Additional repainting work and improved signing was undertaken at Acton Central, Brondesbury, Camden Road, Dalston Junction, Finchley Road & Frognal and West End Lane.

Gale Damage

On the evening of 8th December 1954 a major storm caused extensive damage to the platform canopies at Gunnersbury, injuring several passengers in the process. A temporary canopy was erected and this survived until the rebuilding of the station in the mid-1960s. The old engine shed at South Acton, which had been disused since 1916, was a victim of the same storm and was wholly destroyed.

Collision at South Acton

On Saturday 7th November 1959 thick fog caused considerable disruption across the whole of the south of England. Many sporting events were cancelled in the traditional 'pea-souper' and visibility in the capital was down to ten yards, according to a report in the *Evening Standard*. The 7.25am train from Richmond to Broad Street ploughed into the back of the earlier 7.10am departure from Richmond at South Acton, injuring twelve people. Seats were thrown about inside the unit and many windows broken. The driver of the 7.25 and the guard of the earlier train were both taken to hospital.

End of Austerity

By the end of the 1950s, the railways were beginning to modernise at last. Many schemes had been delayed by the war and the subsequent shortage of materials. The 1960s would bring their own problems and over the next twenty years much of the old NLR system would be fighting for its very existence. The line's traditional traffic would be reduced by the run-down of the docks and the movement of freight to the roads.

Few things proved more vulnerable than canopy glass – if not blown out by blast it was taken out for safety's sake. Willesden High Level, 1953.

Above. Recovery of a sort. Gospel Oak station in 1965 rebuilt and refashioned inside, it is true, but in deeply depressing style. Compare with the earlier photographs of the poor old place.

Left. Kensal Rise station in 1965, an unappetising a prospect as one could think of.

Chapter Fourteen
But a Bleak Outlook ?

The 1960s would herald a period of great change on the railways. Some parts of the old NLR would disappear for ever, while its core would itself be threatened with loss of passenger services. The opening of main trunk roads and the disappearance of the docks would see more change in ten years than in the whole of the previous century. The decade did not begin well, and in October 1962, as part of an economy measure, off-peak services on the Broad Street to Richmond route were reduced from four to three an hour. No trains ran after 9pm.

New trains introduced and old ones withdrawn

The original rolling stock was now ready for withdrawal. New trains, to a standard British Railways design, were ordered in 1955; they were shorter and wider than similar ex-Southern Railway units and were built at Eastleigh Works, with underframe and electrical equipment undertaken at Ashford Works. Fifty-seven three-car sets were built, similar to stock being put into traffic on Tyneside and the Southern Region. They entered service between 1957 and 1959. The slam doors had bars across the droplight windows, to avoid head injuries in Hampstead Heath and Primrose Hill tunnels. From 1969 these units were designated Class 501.

Willesden loses its main line platforms

The closure of Willesden Junction main line platforms on 3rd December 1962, as part of the West Coast Main Line modernisation, isolated the Euston-Watford 'new line' and NLL services from the main services out of Euston. Most buildings and all platforms were demolished shortly after closure, to make room for signalling structures being installed as part of the West Coast updating. Passengers from the north now had to make additional changes at either Watford Junction or Harrow & Wealdstone, or travel to Euston and then back again.

The 'Beeching Report'

In 1963, the 'Beeching' Report, *The Reshaping of British Railways*, was published. It recommended withdrawal of passenger services between Broad Street and Richmond and modification to the Broad Street to Watford Junction service. Under the Beeching Report most of the line would have been retained for freight use, although the report prompted the closure of many of the local freight sidings and goods yards. The report championed the use of containers for freight and as a result, the country's first Freightliner depot was laid out at Maiden Lane goods yard, York Way, in November 1965. This depot was soon unable to cope with the demand for such services, however. The line between Primrose Hill and York Way was electrified at 25kV overhead in two sections, as part of the Euston to Manchester/Liverpool electrification scheme. The first section, from the main line to a point 510 yards on the Camden Road side of Primrose Hill station, was energised on 25th October 1965. The remainder of the route to York Way was similarly treated on 14th November 1966.

Economies and Closures

The link from Bow to Bromley curve was closed to freight traffic on 14th September 1959. Sunday services were withdrawn from South Acton on 1st March 1965, and the station also lost its late evening service. A week later Canonbury, Caledonian Road & Barnsbury and Kentish Town West also saw the Sunday services disappear. As a result, journey times were reduced by five minutes.

Conventional wagon load freight services continued to decline as British Railways was forced to retreat from unprofitable traffic. The Hammersmith & Chiswick branch goods were withdrawn on 3rd May 1965. Since the 1930s this line had been served by only one train, Mondays to Fridays, departing South Acton at 1pm and returning from Hammersmith at 5pm. A great number of goods yards along the NLL closed at this time following implementation of the Beeching report and the end of 'common carrier' status.

The Millwall Dock lines officially closed to freight traffic in 1966, although few trains had run since the early part of the decade.

A Fight for Survival

Local authorities fought the closure plans and one, Hampstead Borough Council, lobbied for the line to be transferred to London Transport as part of the Under-

Kensal Rise in 1961, with Richmond-bound electric unit. The Richmond service was one of the few in London threatened under the Beeching axe and this shadow through the 1960s did much to make the blight on the NLR even worse. A ministerial reprieve came in June 1965.

ground system, as did the well known Liberal MP Jo Grimmond, who lived at Richmond and had first mooted the idea in an article in the *Manchester Guardian* of 8th December 1962. In those days, the single fare from Richmond to Broad Street cost was 2/3d (11p).

Reprieved

After much lobbying by the local authorities and others and a debate in the House of Commons, the threat of passenger train withdrawal was lifted in June 1965, when the Minister of Transport, Tom Fraser, announced the line's reprieve.

Campaigning for re-opening to Poplar

A campaign for the reopening of the Poplar line was soon underway. Local roads were not coping with increasing car ownership. Following a meeting of the Hackney Trades Council in October 1966, a twelve-strong committee of representatives from the Trades Council, the Labour Party and the trade unions was formed to pursue the reopening plan. Sadly, during this period, several of the stations which had closed during the war were demolished and the platforms removed. These included Bow, and the redundant buildings on the disused platforms at Dalston Junction. The track on the former Up line (towards Poplar) from Dalston Junction to Dalston Eastern

Junction was removed during 1965. The Down line between Dalston Junction and Dalston Eastern Junction had been removed in October 1962. This quickly put paid to any reopening proposals almost before they had been mooted. A further reopening campaign for the Dalston to Poplar line began in the early 1970s but like the one some years previously, it came to nothing.

Investment and Improvements

With some sort of future secure, work began on a modest updating of the Broad Street to Richmond line. BR (funded by the Greater London Council) undertook some station improvements by putting in new signs to identify stations from street level, producing full colour route maps and initiating a substantial press and publicity campaign.

Gunnersbury station was rebuilt 1964-67 and a new booking office appeared at Hampstead Heath in the following year, thus completing the rebuilding which had seen the replacement of all platform structures in 1953. New booking offices were also constructed at Caledonian Road & Barnsbury, Canonbury, Dalston Junction, Finchley Road & Frognal and Kensal Rise. In August 1967, coin operated ticket machines were installed on NLL and Euston to Watford local line stations. During the years 1966-70, many stations were

subject to small improvements as part of the 'Minor Station Improvement Scheme'. Old platform buildings, in poor condition and no longer in use, were demolished and replaced with 'Abacus' style shelters, at Brondesbury, Brondesbury Park, Caledonian Road & Barnsbury, Canonbury, Dalston Junction, Finchley Road & Frognal, Kensal Rise, South Acton and West End Lane. West End Lane station was renamed West Hampstead on 5th May 1975, to reflect its close proximity to the West Hampstead Midland station and the nearby Bakerloo (now Jubilee Line) underground station of the same name.

Closure of Kentish Town West

The wooden Kentish Town West station was destroyed by fire on 18th April 1971, the result of an arson attack. As a result services were withdrawn the following day. This station was officially closed on 20th December 1976, though no trains had stopped there since the fire five years earlier. It has since reopened! (on 15 October 1981 - see Chapter 15).

Closure of York Way Freightliner Depot

York Way Freightliner Depot closed in July 1971, just six years after it opened, unable to cope with demand. Most of the traffic was switched to the nearby Willesden Depot.

TO PLATFORMS **4** & **5**

PLATFORM 5 FOR	PLATFORM 4 FOR	
ACTON CENTRAL	KENSAL RISE	KENTISH TOWN WEST
SOUTH ACTON	BRONDESBURY PARK	CAMDEN ROAD
GUNNERSBURY	BRONDESBURY	CALEDONIAN ROAD
KEW GARDENS	WESTEND LANE	HIGHBURY & ISLINGTON
RICHMOND	FINCHLEY ROAD &	CANONBURY
	FROGNAL	DALSTON JUNCTION
	HAMPSTEAD HEATH	BROAD STREET
	GOSPEL OAK	

Broad Street Booking on Point

A new Train Crew Booking On Point was brought into use at Broad Street around 1969, to work the Richmond services with additional crews relocated from Willesden. Watford train crews worked some of the early and late trains to tie in with the movement of units to and from the maintenance depot at Croxley Green. The Booking On Point closed with the station in 1986, when crews were transferred to Watford Junction and Willesden Junction.

Closure Rumours

During 1971, in common with other BR lines, closure rumours abounded. BR denied that there were any such plans, though the London Midland Region admitted that the Broad Street to Richmond line had an annual deficit of £367,000. The North London Line Committee was set up at this time to protect the interests of users, a role the organisation continues to perform today. Meanwhile, the British Road Federation proposed that the line from Hackney Wick to Chalk Farm should be converted to a three lane motorway! The Greater London Council preferred to see the line appearing on underground maps, as it highlighted interchange facilities between the systems. In 1977, the GLC welcomed the inclusion of the NLL on these maps for the first time.

In May 1972, the 'Crosstown Ticket' was introduced as a marketing initiative. At 25p return between any Broad Street to Richmond stations it offered good value. Hardly surprisingly, 12,000 tickets were sold that August.

Willesden Bridge Replacement

The bridges carrying the NLL over the West Coast main line at Willesden Junction were renewed as single line structures over two weekends, 27th-29th March and 10th-12th April 1976. Prior to reconstruction, the up line consisted of a single track bridge; the down line had room for two tracks, though it carried only one originally, serving the additional platform provided for the Earls Court services in 1923.

Freight Loss

During the 1960s, many of the goods facilities at stations were removed, the decline in wagonload freight in favour of bulk trains resulting in the transfer of such business to roads.

Recession and Desperation

By May 1976 the country was in deep recession. As part of the wide-scale economies made by BR at that time, the service frequency on the NLL was reduced from twenty minutes to thirty. The GLC agreed a grant of £150,000 later in the year in order to reinstate the twenty minute interval for twelve months. The situation had become desperate. Passenger figures continued to dwindle on all but the heavily used section between Willesden Junction and Highbury & Islington, and closure yet again reared its ugly head.

Above. **More warm inviting prospects for the 1960s passenger – at Willesden this time, 22 July 1965.**

Left. **Willesden up in the sunshine, 1953 – derelict Kensington platform on right.**

In a sadly denuded Broad Street, on 18 July 1983, the 11.35am train for Richmond leaves with Class 501 DTS (Driver Trailing Standard) vehicle No.75151 leading. Flanking it are two further units of the same type. Photograph Brian Morrison.

Diesel multiple unit made up of cars 54122 and 53364 at Camden Road on 29 October 1984, forming the 15.24 train to Custom House. Photograph Colin J. Marsden.

Chapter Fifteen
New hope, new life

While the North London Line entered the 1970s with little hope for its future, developments over the next two decades would result not only in the securing of that future but considerable, unexpected, expansion.

'Ring Rail'
The promotion of an outer circle, or 'Ring Rail' as it became known, was first promoted in 1974, by MP Nigel Spearing (Newham South) amongst others. This envisaged the reopening of the line from Dalston Western Junction to Stratford, using the North Woolwich line as far as Silvertown, together with a new tunnel under the Thames to Woolwich where it would join up with the Southern Region. The line would continue to Clapham Junction where the West London Line (WLL) would be reopened to Willesden Junction; after that trains would take the NLL again back to Dalston, thus completing the circle. New life was breathed into the NLL from the GLC's *London Rail Study* of 1974. This report devoted a section to orbital services and recommended upgrading lines in North London to provide a network of non-radial services:
Broad Street - Richmond
North Woolwich - Stratford - West Hamp-
stead - Willesden Junction - Ealing Broad-
way - Greenford
Barking - Gospel Oak - West Hampstead -
Willesden Junction - Clapham Junction
After the manner of such things, most of these schemes fell by the wayside, yet they would continue to influence thinking over the next twenty years and allow some of the plans to reach fruition in the two decades that followed.

Investment Plans
In February 1978 BR Chairman Sir Peter Parker, addressing the City of Westminster Chamber of Commerce, announced improvements to the North London Line. These included some much-needed investment in the Stratford to North Woolwich line and its integration with a reopened service from Dalston to Stratford. The renovated section was to include new stations serving the Dalston, Hackney and Homerton areas. Sir Peter expressed hopes that this work would provide the first steps to creating an electric orbital railway from North Woolwich to Richmond. As a result, the line from Dalston Western Junction to Stratford was upgraded for passenger use. Initially the stations planned for Hackney were to be known as 'Mare Street' and 'Wallis Road'. Within a short time they were re-classified on planning documents as 'Hackney Central' and 'Hackney Wick'. The GLC was by now actively pursuing (in the terminology of the time) a pro-active public transport policy and its 1978-79 Transport Committee budget included provision for building the three identified stations on the reopened Dalston to Stratford section - Dalston Kingsland, Hackney Central and Hackney Wick.

Better times for Stratford - North Woolwich
Train services between Stratford and North Woolwich were replaced by buses over the period 18th-22nd September 1978 to allow for extensive modifications to the track at Silvertown and other stations. A new station building was erected at North Woolwich, utilising part of the old goods yard, releasing the old station building for other uses. One platform was lengthened to accommodate six coach trains. At the same time, Silvertown, Custom House and Canning Town were rebuilt in the BR architectural house style of the period. The new building at Canning Town was the fifth to serve the area.

Part of the 'price' to be paid for the North London's survival was the stripping away of much of the original station architecture – most of it of course in appalling condition. It gave way to poor quality, unappealing 'bus shelter' stuff such as this. It effectively removed such stations from the 'townscape' in which they had previously sat so well. This is Dalston Junction on 3 July 1979 with the 10.17 am Broad Street-Richmond arriving. The sets were by now 'Class 501'; the leading car is DTS No.M75186. Photograph Brian Morrison.

clearance tests in April 1982. The tests were run from Liverpool Street to Broxbourne, to ensure the units' third rail collection shoes would not foul the trackwork or anything else, should the line from Graham Road to Liverpool Street be installed and the Broad Street closure enforced.

Broad Street's demise was approved by the Secretary of State for Transport, David Howell, in February 1983, though this was dependent on the provision of a temporary platform at Worship Street (just outside Broad Street) until trains could get access to Liverpool Street itself. A bus link was planned from Worship Street to Liverpool Street during this period. By this time, passengers using the station had declined to a mere 3,300 per day. No actual closure date was agreed but by the time of implementation, the temporary arrangements were no longer needed and trains worked into Broad Street.

There was opposition to the closure of Broad Street and as part of its campaign, the Railway Development Society held a publicity event on board a train from Richmond to Broad Street and also at the terminus itself. The London Regional Passengers Committee (LRPC) also opposed the closure, calling for the Graham Road curve to be double track and for high level platforms to be installed at Liverpool Street.

North Woolwich joins the NLL
Services had begun running from Camden Road to North Woolwich, utilising the reopened route east of Dalston Western Junction, on 14th May 1979. Operated initially by diesel multiple units, the intermediate stations on the reopened Dalston-Stratford section were still unfinished. These units used a 'layover' siding at Hampstead Road, to avoid blocking the lines through Camden Road between arrival and departure time, although it was not unknown for them to remain on the running lines between Camden Road and Primrose Hill stations. A new station was provided at West Ham, coming into use on the opening day, to effect interchange with the District Line of London Underground. Hackney Wick and Hackney Central stations were opened a year later, on 12th May 1980, with BR Chairman Sir Peter Parker and Leader of the GLC, Horace Cutler, officiating. Within a month of the stations being opened, Hackney Public Transport Action Committee were questioning the siting of these new stations and criticising ticketing arrangements.

Investment Implemented
June 1980 saw ML Engineering of Plymouth awarded a contract to carry out alterations at Richmond signal box, so

Dalston Junction, as scruffy as a platform can get, 3 June 1979. The train is the 09.30 Richmond-Broad Street, M61156 leading. Photograph Brian Morrison.

'No.1' lines closed
The freight lines from Canonbury Junction to Camden Road were taken out of use in September 1981 and closed officially on 5th October that year – this was attributed to the deteriorating condition of the track over Randolph Street, Baynes Street and Pancras Way. The condition of Bridge No.105 at York Way also inhibited use of the line, and vehicles with 25 ton axleloads were restricted to the electrified 'No.2' lines. Although out of use, the 'No.1' non-electrified lines were 'mothballed' in case additional traffic warranted reinstatement. Some sections of track were later removed, but most were left in place.

Broad Street Decline Continues
In January 1979, the independent North London Line Committee stated that only 20% of peak hour NLL passengers used Broad Street. This was the first indication that services into Broad Street might be diverted or abandoned in favour of other routes. Eventually, the Broad Street line (it was said) could eventually be closed and services diverted into Liverpool Street via a newly constructed curve at Graham Road, Hackney. This brought the highly attractive prospect of prime development land in the heart of the City (now Broadgate) which would fund the rebuilding of Liverpool Street station with little inconvenience to Broad Street commuters.

As part of the closure plans, a Class 47 locomotive hauling a 501 electric unit (No. 501 154, of the type then in use on North London d.c. services) conducted that it could take over the Gunnersbury box operations, with the western section of the line under the control of one box. The redundant 22 lever frame from Gunnersbury was installed in a new box on the independent Swanage Railway at Harmans Cross, during the summer of 1995.

Electrification Approved
Nearly a year later, the GLC Transport Committee approved in principle a £10.3 million grant for electrification of the Dalston to North Woolwich route, using the 3rd rail system. Ken Livingstone, then Leader of the GLC, reopened Kentish Town West station on 5th October 1981. The £400,000 cost of rebuilding was funded entirely by the GLC. Exactly a year after draft approval, in April 1982, the Council gave full approval for the electrification of the line from Dalston to North Woolwich.

Gospel Oak for Barking
Originally Barking services over the THJR ran in and out of St. Pancras but by the 1950s most trains to Barking and East Ham originated from Kentish Town station on the Midland main line. Services could still run to St. Pancras when required, although this was no longer possible from the early 1960s, when an empty sleeping car train from St. Pancras to Cricklewood split the point lock at Islip Street Junction. One bogie stayed on the main line while a second took the line towards Barking. The signal box controlling the junction was demolished in the collision and the junction itself badly damaged.

As part of the Midland Suburban Electrification Scheme (St. Pancras to Bedford), the Barking to Kentish Town service was diverted to Gospel Oak from 5th January 1981. The former Tottenham & Hampstead platform at Gospel Oak (abandoned since it was last used for special trains, in 1939) was resited for the purpose. The work also involved the rebuilding of the junction from the Midland main line to the Barking line, from the north. The integration of the Barking line into the NLL services greatly increased journey opportunities.

The London & South East Sector
As part of its policy to sectorise its disparate services into businesses, the London & South East (L&SE) sector of BR was formed on 4th January 1982, to look after its commuter interests in and around London. One of three passenger businesses formed at that time (the others were InterCity and Provincial (later Regional Railways), it provided one body to co-ordinate the ever-more demanding requirements for travel to and from the capital.

The headquarters of the new organisation were located at Waterloo's General Offices alongside those of the Southern Region. Its Director also served, at that time, as the Southern's General Manager and it is not surprising that Waterloo influences were to the fore. Despite its many critics, the SR was an extremely efficient network, having far more suburban routes than the other Regions. It was this organisation, L&SE, that developed the Dalston to North Woolwich electrification scheme and funded the extensive 'North London Link' marketing campaign that went with it.

Fire at Acton Central
The canopy on the Down (Richmond bound) platform was ruined by fire on 17th February 1981. It was subsequently demolished in 1990, a victim of rot, although complete removal of the adjacent buildings was stopped following intervention by the London Borough of Ealing. The remaining structures were made safe but offered little respite from the elements, although a small wooden shelter was built away from the canopy. The local authority meanwhile, continued to lobby for reinstatement of the full canopy, having refused planning permission for new ones. Now a conservation area, only 'like-for-like' replacement was considered acceptable.

End of the Poplar line?
British Rail closed the line to Poplar on 5th October 1981, with remaining traffic (it had fallen to 26,500 tons a year – largely imported steel from the continent, export steel to the United States and malt to Africa) redirected to the rail-served docks at either Grays or Purfleet. The last BR train down the line ran on 9th February 1984, a diesel multiple unit carrying engineers investigating the proposed light railway system for Docklands, the Docklands Light Railway (DLR). All track was lifted by 13th May 1985.

The former main line from Bow to Poplar, abandoned that year, was incorporated into the DLR's Stratford-Poplar line. The DLR used several sections of abandoned British Rail track

Freight was ever the lifeblood of the North London and it serves today, still, as an invaluable artery 'crossing the grain' of the main lines in the South East. Two 56 diesels (56049 and 56035) rattle the greenhouse panes and rustle the back garden shrubbery near Hampstead Heath on 15 October 1984, with the 10.21 Purfleet-Merehead ballast empties. Photograph Colin J. Marsden.

On 6 and 7 June 1984 Southern 2EPBs Nos.6309 and 5773 operated a series of specials to test the conductor rail gaps between Richmond and Broad Street, Watford and Euston. Here it is approaching Willesden en route from Broad Street to Watford via Primrose Hill. The North London landscape changed again and again. Willesden for instance was fields and meadows at one time, became 'respectable' and then slowly slid down the social scale. Alterations in the railway working of the huge junction, contraction and all manner of modern building left a range of structures, widely separated in time and sitting uneasily one with the other. This process is typical of much of the North London Line hinterland. Photograph Colin J. Marsden.

bed including the former London and Blackwall section between Tower Gateway and east of Westferry. The line from Bow to Victoria Park remains abandoned. The proposals for the DLR were lodged with Parliament in November 1983 and approved the following year. The initial routes from Tower Gateway to Poplar and Stratford - Poplar - Island Gardens were opened by H.M. The Queen on 30th July 1987.

More Stations Reopened
A new station at Dalston Kingsland opened on 16th May 1983, on the site of the station which closed in 1865. The official opening took place the following day, when Dave Wetzel, Chairman of the GLC Transport Committee, officiated. The station had been rebuilt at a cost of £650,000 of which £166,000 had been met by grants from the GLC and Department of Transport's Environment Urban Programme. The reopening of Homerton station (closed in 1945) was approved by the GLC Transport Committee in January 1984. The cost, £440,000, was sponsored by Hackney Partnership Scheme. The station reopened on 13th May 1985.

The End of the Silvertown Tramway
The Silvertown Tramway was progres-

sively cut back from west to east as industry withdrew from the area and the decline of the docks continued. The sidings at the Silvertown end, however, remained to serve the scrap yard of Thomas Ward Ltd. Trains of scrap metal ran from these sidings until 1986, using a long head shunt towards North Woolwich and a second freight only line from the head shunt, through the Connaught Tunnel, to Custom House. The signal box at Custom House was destroyed by fire in 1985.

North Woolwich becomes a Railway Museum
The old terminus building at North Woolwich was transferred to the GLC for it to be transformed into a railway museum concentrating mainly on the GER, a 'branch' of the Passmore Edwards Museum. It opened officially on 20th November 1984, Her Majesty The Queen Mother travelling on a special train to the opening hauled by LNER A3 Pacific No. 4472 'Flying Scotsman'.

Southern Region Units on Test
With work on the electrification east of Dalston proceeding, tests were carried out using Class 416/3 (Southern Region 2EPB) units to see if they were suitable

for the route. In January 1985, it was confirmed that these units would be introduced from the start of electrified services to North Woolwich. Like the Class 501s they replaced, fifteen units were prepared with safety bars on the droplight windows.

25kV electrification of the 'No.1' lines
BR's Railfreight sector made a £12 million submission on 1st November 1984, to electrify the line from Camden Road to Stratford at 25kV overhead, at the same time reinstating some of the former 'No.1' lines between Maiden Lane and Canonbury Junction. Under-Secretary of State for Transport, David Mitchell MP, gave his approval to the scheme the following month.

Tunnel trouble and Signal Box Fire
On 2nd December 1984 the retaining wall at the east end of Hampstead Heath Tunnel (near Hampstead Heath station) collapsed, prompting local fears that this would lead to permanent closure of this section. Major engineering work was quickly organised but even so, through services did not resume until 15th April 1985. In the early hours of 11th March 1985 Gospel Oak signal box had been con-

sumed by fire. *The Hampstead & Highgate Express* of 15th March reported that the likely cause was an electrical fault. Sadly, the Signalman died in the fire. The closure of the line for repairs to the tunnel was utilised by the engineers for a number of other improvements – shortening and rebuilding of platforms at Kensal Rise, West Hampstead, Hampstead Heath, Brondesbury and Brondesbury Park. Track was also relaid and Kensal Green Junction remodelled. During the disruption, services initially ran from Richmond to Finchley Road & Frognal and from Broad Street to Gospel Oak. A bus service operated between Finchley Road and Gospel Oak stations. Later on, the Broad Street service ran to Willesden Junction Low Level via Primrose Hill and the North Woolwich diesel service was extended to Gospel Oak.

Electrification Complete

A little over eight miles, the line from Dalston Junction to North Woolwich was officially opened to electric traction on 14th May 1985, by former West Ham and England footballer, Trevor Brooking, MBE. A special train was organised to convey the guests from North Woolwich to Richmond, stopping en route at Homerton for Cllr. Kenrick Hanson, the Mayor of Hackney, to undertake the official reopening ceremony (the station actually had opened for services the previous day). The electrification project was completed on time at a cost of £7.1m, a considerable saving over the original budget costs of £10.3m.

May 1985 also saw the completion of electrification of the North London Incline at 25kV, from the NLL near Camden Road to the East Coast Main Line close to the Copenhagen Tunnels, via Kings Cross goods yard. This work was undertaken to allow empty stock movement of Class 313s between the Watford-Euston line and their then home depot of Hornsey. The extension of electrified services beyond Dalston to North Woolwich was soon furnishing figures to justify the work – by July 1985, the NLL was showing an 80% increase in traffic levels.

Work progressed on the 25kV overhead electrification of the 'No.1' lines from Camden Road to Dalston Western Junction and over the remaining double track section to Stratford. Also included in this project was the old GNR line from Finsbury Park to Canonbury East Junction. Tracks were shared with the passenger services between Dalston Western Junction and Channelsea Junction, Stratford which thus became a dual voltage section (25kV overhead line and 650v d.c. 3rd rail). The whole of this was commissioned on 11th November 1987, six months ahead of schedule. A through InterCity express ran from Glasgow to Harwich Parkeston Quay via Birmingham (and vice-versa) over the route from May 1987 to May 1988. For a while, the Glasgow train changed locomotives at Camden Road. This could have provided a useful service but as it was not shown in the timetable, no tickets could be sold!

Liverpool Street and Broadgate

As early as June 1975 BR had revealed plans for rebuilding Liverpool Street station. The old Liverpool Street was to be swept away and replaced by a modern structure of 22 platforms. Conservationists, led by Poet Laureate Sir John Betjeman, were horrified and a preservation society was formed. The society went on to outline ways in which Liverpool Street station could be radically improved, without the wholesale destruction of the main architectural features.

The cost of such a major rebuilding was high. With trains from Broad Street being diverted to either North Woolwich or Liverpool Street itself (as already outlined) the prime development land released by demolition of Broad Street station could be used to fund the Liverpool Street project. These plans required Parliamentary approval and the Liverpool Street Modernisation Bill received the Royal Assent in April 1983.

The end in sight for Broad Street

The newly electrified line to North Woolwich resulted in a large reduction in the number of trains serving Broad Street, which by now was served only by a handful of trains from Watford Junction via Primrose Hill. Between 29th July and 23rd August 1985, Cambridge Heath station on the Liverpool Street to Enfield Town line was closed between 10.00 and 16.00, facilitating the construction of the Graham Road curve and allowing trains access to Liverpool Street from the NNL at Dalston Kingsland.

Willesden again. Set 501170 departs Willesden Junction for Broad Street, 6 June 1984. Photograph Colin J. Marsden.

A Class 501 electric multiple unit crosses the Western Region main line near Acton Wells Junction, on 17 August 1983. Photograph Brian Morrison.

Broadgate Plans Revised

The redevelopment of the Broad Street site was still causing controversy. In early 1985, BR invited property developers to submit further ideas, Rosehaugh Stanhope Developments emerging with the winning scheme. Work began on the first stage with the station still open, utilising areas no longer in use. In July 1985 the Prime Minister, Margaret Thatcher, officiated at the start of work ceremony. She returned a year later to open the first of the impressive new buildings. This work required demolition of the great part of Broad Street station, with a temporary extension to an existing platform, reached via Sun Street Passage.

End of the Class 501s

The last of the Class 501 units was withdrawn from service on 2nd October 1985. Vehicles Nos.M70170 and M75186 were sold to the Marchwood Military Railway in Hampshire. In 1972, Wolverton Works (British Rail Engineering Limited) was awarded a contract for converting two Class 501 Motor Open Brake Second surplus vehicles to battery operated locomotives for use on the Merseyrail electrification scheme, in and around Liverpool. This involved major tunnel work under the centre of Liverpool, and diesels were barred because of fumes. These battery locomotives became DB975178 and DB975179 respectively.

Eight more surplus vehicles were converted to battery locomotives at Doncaster Works, four for use at Hornsey in 1975 and four for Cricklewood in 1980.

All ten had been withdrawn by British Rail by July 1993.

Broad Street Closes

On 30th June 1986, shortly after the formation of Network SouthEast (NSE), the line from Dalston Western Junction to Broad Street was finally closed. The Graham Road curve opened on the same day, allowing the diversion of the remaining Watford Junction to Broad Street trains into the adjacent Liverpool Street with dual voltage (AC/DC) Class 313 units, and the closure of both Broad Street and Dalston Junction stations. Within a short period, the area on which Broad Street had stood had been cleared by the demolition contractors.

Broadgate Opens

Within eighteen months of the closure of Broad Street, the Prince of Wales was able to participate in a major ceremony to officially open the Broadgate scheme. The developers had wisely included large public areas, shops, restaurants and an outdoor ice rink, the only one in Britain. These have become very popular with those who work nearby. At the opening ceremony, Prince Charles was able to watch a skating demonstration by Torvill and Dean on the new rink.

Broadgate concentrated on constructing buildings designed to provide quality accommodation for financial and other institutions. With the widespread introduction of computer based technology, many of these firms relocated from buildings no longer able to cope with the technical needs of such activities. The

success of the Broadgate development was that it benefited from being in 'the right place at the right time'.

Class 416s Take Over

The Southern Region Class 416/3s were two-car versions of the more common Class 415 4EPB third rail electric multiple units. Fitted with Electro Pneumatic Brake (hence the EPB designation) and automatic buckeye couplers, these units first appeared from Eastleigh Works in the 1950s. The two-car versions were built in 1959 and the first examples were based on SR Bulleid designs; later versions utilised the BR Mark One coach body shell. These 416/3 units were drafted on to the North London Line as part of the centralisation of the fleet operated by the then London & South East Sector of British Rail. Fifteen were fitted with window bars for working through Hampstead Heath tunnel, and were only used on the Richmond to North Woolwich route between 1985 and 1989 before returning to their former territory, south of the river. During their time on the NLL, they were allocated and maintained at Selhurst Depot, Croydon. Although carrying various liveries during their working lives, they only appeared in the then BR corporate blue/grey during their period on the NLL.

The Network SouthEast Era

In January 1986, ScotRail's energetic General Manager, Chris Green, was appointed Director of the London & SouthEast sector of BR. Chris Green had made the Scottish Region BR's most efficient operation over the 1984-86 period. This was achieved by aggressive marketing, emphasising customer care and creating the ScotRail image. Within days of his arrival, it became apparent to all those who worked at Waterloo that exciting times were on the way. Whilst such events are outside the real scope of this book, they amounted to the biggest shake-up of London's railways for many a year. Within six months, on 10th June 1986, Network SouthEast was enthusiastically launched at Waterloo, a new name, new livery and new organisation which broke down Regional boundaries to give 'One Railway for London'. It was decided that the assembled guests would take the newly liveried NSE Class 455 unit to Richmond to view the refurbishing of the 1935 station. NSE was an instant success and a new and vibrant chapter in London's railway story was unfolding.

With NSE now giving a higher profile to London's railways, coupled with the introduction of the Capitalcard (now Travelcard), which gave unlimited access to trains, buses and tube trains within the zoned areas, the North London Line was again proving popular. The 'Ministers Cup', first presented by Minister of Transport David Mitchell, in October 1986, was instituted for the NSE route which showed the best overall performance improvement. The North London Line was the second route to be presented with the trophy, which was awarded at six monthly intervals.

In January 1987 Chris Green outlined his aspirations for the North London, when discussing NSE's ten year business plan. He indicated his wishes to see Class 456 'Clipper' (the 'Clipper' name was not adopted, and the 456s eventually entered service on the South London Line) units drafted on to the line in the future. This class was one of several then in the design and development stage by NSE's traction and rolling stock team.

The North London Lines of Network SouthEast

In May 1989 the NSE's six divisions were reorganised into nine. 'Line Branding' (an effort to give a controlled approach to some of the enthusiastic, but unofficial, 'brands') was introduced at the same time. The North London was one of nineteen 'branded' lines so created (they were subsequently reduced to fifteen), incorporating the Euston to Watford local services, Richmond to North Woolwich, Gospel Oak to Barking, Watford Junction to Croxley Green and Watford Junction to St. Albans Abbey lines.

The NLL logo was based on the triangles of the Harlequin's costume, adopted earlier for the Euston to Watford local service which had been similarly marketed as the 'Harlequin Line' from the summer of 1988. This name had been derived from HAtch End, HARLEsden and QUeens Park stations and was chosen following a competition, won by Simon Gurevitz of Harrow. 'Harlequin'

was also chosen for the large shopping development in Watford which runs adjacent to the line, and is well served from Watford High Street station.

The NSE policy of 'total route modernisation' began to take effect. Some, like the Marylebone to Aylesbury and Banbury lines with their ageing semaphore signalling and diesel multiple units, were completely transformed. Such a scheme would have benefited the North London and although Network managers fought for it, it was not to be. The 'boom' of the 1980s was coming to an end. The country was now in recession and jobs were being lost. The political mood was also changing and the words 'privatisation' and 'reorganisation' used with increasing regularity.

NSE classified its 944 stations in categories from A to E. For each group a 'flagship' station for refurbishment was identified, so that the scheme could be evaluated before further work was undertaken. Brondesbury Park was chosen as the 'flagship' category D station and the refurbishment proved highly successful. It set the standards for implementation at the other NLL stations. To mark the completion of the work a ceremony was held at the station on 10th July 1989. To complement the Brondesbury Park work, new booking offices were built at Camden Road. Improved waiting facilities were provided at Gospel Oak and Willesden Junction (High Level). Other works followed at South Acton, Kew Gardens,

A **Class 501 set crosses the grand Union canal at Old Oak Common on 12 May 1980,** with the inevitable Broad Street-Richmond service. Photograph Colin J. Marsden.

Gospel Oak and Hampstead Heath. In October 1989, a Route Manager was appointed to take control of the 22 miles 20 chains of the NLL which, up until then, had been organised between three Network Managers, three Regions, four Area Managers and six Train Crew Depots. All rolling stock maintenance and cleaning was undertaken away from the line at Selhurst Depot, Croydon. The creation of the new organisation had a dramatic effect. All slam door stock was replaced by dual voltage Class 313s, squeezed from other parts of NSE's fleet by determination and hard work. In an effort to raise the profile of the line, the NLL held a gala week in the autumn of 1989.

Class 313 units replace EPBs
As related above, the Class 416/3 EPB units were replaced in 1989 by dual voltage Class 313 units from elsewhere in the NSE fleet. They had been built for the Great Northern Electrification and dated from 1976-78. They were the first units to have an aluminium body shell and were based on the 'PEP' prototype vehicles. The 313s were also the first to be fitted with 'Tightlock' couplings which, as well as coupling the vehicles together, incorporate all air and electrical connections, thus avoiding the use of ugly cables on the front of units. This equipment has been used on subsequent modern electric multiple units.

Originally 64 units were built, based at Hornsey. From 1985 a number were put to work on the Watford-Euston line and from 1989 additional units, fitted with additional collector shoes, were supplied to work the Richmond-North Woolwich services. They carried NSE livery from 1986 onwards; for maintenance purposes a number later transferred from Hornsey to Bletchley.

Following privatisation, the Class 313 units passed to Eversholt Leasing Company, with twenty-three three-car units being leased by NLRlys. (See next chapter. To avoid confusion with the original NLR referred to throughout the book, the later North London Railways operations will be shown as NLRlys.) Since modernisation of the Richmond to North Woolwich line, the dual voltage capability has been well utilised. Following completion of the West London Line electrification, they have appeared on Willesden Junction-Clapham Junction services.

A programme of mid-life refurbishment began in 1997, with extensive work on mechanical and electrical components, as well as the interiors, doors and bodywork. This is currently being carried out at Adtranz, Ilford, the units returning after extensive rebuilding in the purple, green and yellow colours of Silverlink Train Services. They continue to be allocated to Bletchley and are expected to remain in service for some considerable time. All Class 313 units were trans-

formed, in a programme completed by the end of 1999.

A new station for Silvertown
Silvertown station was rebuilt in the late 1980s as part of the development of Docklands, which included the creation of the new 'London City' Airport on derelict dock land. The rebuilt station became Silvertown & London City Airport and was opened by Michael Portillo MP on 7th October 1989.

Towards the 1990s
The rejuvenation of the NLL had been dramatic during the 1980s and it entered the 1990s as the lynchpin around which further developments could take place.

Top right. **Denuded platforms at Dalston Junction on 3 June 1979. The train is empty, a morning peak working from Richmond going back to Croxley Green. Photograph Brian Morrison.**

Below. **Class 501 set No.157 passes Western Junction box, Dalston, with the 10.34am Broad Street-Richmond train, 15 October 1984. A DMU sits in the re-opened Dalston Kingsland platforms. Photograph Colin J. Marsden.**

Richmond on 20 September 1985, and an LT train leaves for Upminster at 11.21am. Photograph Colin J. Marsden.

Crossing the canal bridge between Willesden High Level and Acton Wells Junction on 15 April 1987 is Class 416/3 2EPB No.6323, forming the 11.37am North Woolwich-Richmond service. Photograph Brian Morrison.

Railway abandonment means empty space, and for long such scars could be found punctuating the NL. Class 56 No.56036 hauls empty ARC hoppers between Willesden High Level and Acton Wells Junction, 15 April 1987. Photograph Brian Morrison.

Chapter Sixteen
Great Changes

Network SouthEast Takes Control

In April 1992, the former Regional organisations were abolished. NSE now had complete control of its own services instead of just the marketing. But, instead of reaping a just glory, the moment it had implemented the scheme that could deliver the 'One Railway for London' dream, NSE instead looked forward only to a premature demise. Coupled with the departure of Chris Green, who moved on to head the prestigious InterCity organisation, NSE embarked on a period of great change, in line with the Government's privatisation plans. Each of the nine divisions took more control of their own organisations and the former uniform approach no longer held sway.

Liverpool Street Services Withdrawn

While growth continued on the Richmond to North Woolwich corridor, there was a gradual decline in the Liverpool Street services. On diversion into Liverpool Street in June 1986 there had been eleven trains each way; from 2nd October 1989, this was reduced to one peak period return each way. The London Regional Passengers' Committee held a Public Hearing on 31st October 1991 to air objections to the proposed withdrawal of the remaining Watford to Liverpool Street service but despite protests, this was withdrawn on 28th September 1992, with Primrose Hill station closing the same day. The last train left Liverpool Street at 17.52 but, due to flooding was diverted via Hampstead Heath and did not call at Primrose Hill for the final time!

A real main line at last?

The failure to build the Channel Tunnel Rail Link (CTRL) during the period the tunnel was under construction left the railway operators with a problem. The only way of carrying the hoped-for traffic levels was to upgrade existing lines leading to the tunnel. This was to result in a major modernisation scheme for both the West London Line and NLL, to enable the Eurostar 'North of London' services to gain access to both the east and west coast main lines.

Funded by BR's European Passenger Services (EPS – operators of Eurostar trains) BR embarked on a two year £60m modernisation scheme for the NLL in October 1993. Not only would the improvements benefit international travellers but local users too. The modernisation allowed for the upgrading of the entire line from South Acton to Camden Road, so that the route could be used by EPS Eurostar trains operating beyond London. Publicised under the 'Towards Tomorrow' banner, work on this section included:

Replacement of the 3rd rail electrification system between South Acton and Camden Road with 25kV overhead and the removal of the former system. The dual voltage Class 313 units operating on the line can therefore work from both systems.

Track renewals, realignment and platform clearance work.

Replacement of three footbridges over the railway at South Acton, Acton Central and Acton Wells.

Refurbishment of Hampstead Heath tunnel, including extensive lowering of the track bed which would be constructed of concrete, and installation of 25kV overhead line equipment.

Gunnersbury station, heavily vandalised and frequently attacked by graffiti gangs, badly needed refurbishment at this time and this work too, was to be undertaken. The adjacent office block was acquired for the new headquarters of the British Standard Institution (BSI) and this organisation agreed to fund station work as part of the development.

A Richmond-North Woolwich service near Acton Wells Junction, 15 April 1987. The train is the 11.45am, formed of Class 416/3 2EPB No.6322. Photograph Brian Morrison.

Class 416/3 2EPB No.6328, forming the 8.42 Saturdays Only Richmond-North Woolwich, near Caledonian Road & Barnsbury on 21 May 1988. Photograph Brian Morrison.

'Expanding the Horizons'

The NSE's North Division launched its 'Expanding The Horizons' scheme in the autumn of 1993. Aimed at publicising the potential of the NLL following modernisation, it outlined plans to reopen the WLL and to rebuild Willesden Junction into the hub of the system. The former up and down slow line platforms would be reinstated to greatly improve interchange between the two separate systems. The plan also identified new station sites at Old Oak Common, Kings Cross North, Chiswick Business Park and a number of options for new stations on a reopened WLL. The document enabled discussion to take place with local authorities, transport officials and others keen to unlock the potential of the orbital routes further.

The publication of 'Expanding the Horizons' coincided with the privatisation of British Rail then passing through the House of Commons. As a result some of these plans have not progressed beyond the discussion stage, although they may possibly do so at some time in the future. As we have seen, when it comes to transport planning issues, the process can be lengthy. Some of the issues outlined in the 1974 documents (see Chapter 15) took twenty years to reach fruition.

North London Railways and Railtrack

The Railways Act 1993 became law on 5th November 1993 and resulted in the break up of the NSE empire. On 31st March 1994 the operators of the passenger train services previously run by NSE's North Division were renamed North London Railways (NLRlys), which remained a wholly owned subsidiary of the British Railways Board. Shortly afterwards the new operating company increased the number of trains from three an hour to four in each direction. These plans, of course, were already well in hand before the changeover. Meanwhile, all rolling stock passed to new leasing companies whilst Railtrack assumed responsibility for the infrastructure, i.e. stations and signalling. Railtrack is also responsible for the pathing of trains and for the selling of train paths to the various operators.

The West London Line (WLL)

The West London Line (WLL) reopened to local passenger traffic (between Kensington Olympia and Willesden Junction) on 27th May 1994. From the same day, the Clapham Junction-Kensington Olympia (peak hours only) shuttle service, often referred to as the 'Kenny Belle' was incorporated in the new all day service and became part of the North London Lines of NLRlys. The first section of the WLL had opened 150 years before, to the day, on 27th May 1844.

The fortunes of the line fluctuated after the Second World War and extensive bomb damage in October 1940 had resulted in the withdrawal of the local passenger trains, including the LPTB service from the Hammersmith & City line. Only the Kensington-Clapham Junction section was reinstated and despite much campaigning, it would take 54 years for Kensington Olympia to Willesden Junction to reopen to passenger traffic. The modernisation scheme would include 25kV electrification of the Mitre Bridge-Willesden Junction (High Level Junction) section and, after an initial twelve month period of diesel multiple working, allow for the new service to be operated by dual voltage Class 313 electric multiple units

A Change of Plan

Completion of the modernisation scheme in the summer of 1996 would allow European Passenger Services to commence running two Eurostar trains a day in each direction, from Brussels and Paris to east coast destinations such as Peterborough, York, Newcastle and Edinburgh. Access to and from the East Coast Main Line was made via the WLL, NLL and the North London incline (ECML), east of Camden Road.

In August 1994, however, NLRlys and Railtrack produced a leaflet announcing the postponement of the Hampstead Heath Tunnel work. This had been scheduled for a sixteen week closure to allow the task to be undertaken. The Hampstead Heath work was the keystone on which the remainder of the project was dependent. Its postponement led to much speculation in the media concerning the future of the modernisation project and how Eurostar trains would reach the East Coast Main Line to serve destinations north of London. The absence of electrification on the missing link from Mitre Bridge to Willesden High Level Junction would also have implications for the reinstated WLL services, requiring the extended use of diesel multiple units beyond the anticipated twelve month period. Eurostar services to the West Coast Main Line would not be affected by this decision, gaining access on to the route via West London Junction, close to the old Willesden main line station. This route from Mitre Bridge to West London Junction had been electrified in the 1960s, with the Mitre Bridge-Westway Bridge (A40) section following in 1993.

Some of the modernisation work was completed, however, before the work stopped. The trackbed was realigned and new track laid between South Acton and Willesden Junction High Level. New footbridges were provided at South Acton and Acton Wells to take the 25kV overhead lines. Gunnersbury station was refurbished and a public address system installed throughout the system.

Jubilee Line Extension Work Begins

The Jubilee Line Extension, from Green Park to Stratford via Bermondsey and Docklands, received Royal Assent in March 1992. The Government announced its building on 19th October 1993, and the work required closure of the NLRlys line between Stratford and North Woolwich for a twelve month period, which commenced on 29th May 1994. While only the Canning Town-Stratford

section was affected, the whole of the Stratford-North Woolwich section had to be closed to allow work to take place and replacement buses were drafted into the area, painted in a special NLRlys livery. These buses were operated under contract by Kentish Bus and were paid for by London Underground (LUL). The arrangements included a peak hour double decker express service via Plaistow (Underground station) and, because of the low bridge carrying the LTS/District Line at West Ham, an all-stations service using single deck vehicles.

This enabled the Extension engineers to take over the trackbed completely between Stratford and Canning Town and move over the NLL to accommodate the Jubilee Extension alongside. The stations at West Ham and Canning Town were demolished, to be replaced by new structures to serve both systems – at Canning Town facilities were also provided for the Docklands Light Railway. Work began on 29th May 1994, with the demolition of stations and the lifting of the existing trackwork. Work on constructing the new Canning Town station began on a site close to the original Barking Road station. Both stations, West Ham and Canning Town, reopened with the line on 29th May 1995. Canning Town included a new bus depot along with its NLRlys/DLR and Jubilee Line interchange. The first section of the Jubilee Line Extension opened to passenger traffic on 14th May 1999. The Extension runs from Green Park to Stratford, where it would terminate alongside the NLL platforms at a new western concourse. Between Canning Town and Stratford the JLE runs alongside the NLL tracks on

the former freight lines alignment. A new maintenance depot was constructed on the site of the old Stratford fruit and vegetable market.

Stratford Low Level station buildings were demolished during 1996, although the station platforms remained in use throughout, with a temporary arrangement for passengers to reach the platforms. The new western concourse opened on 14th May 1999. Railtrack subsequently rebuilt the remainder of the station, providing the eastern concourse (which revised arrangements for entering and leaving the station) and making considerable improvements to the cross platform interchanges. Work on realigning the tracks took longer than estimated and the line between Stratford and North Woolwich did not reopen to passenger traffic until 29th October 1995.

The Docklands Light Railway Beckton Extension

The extension of the Docklands Light Railway (DLR) from Poplar to Beckton opened on 28th March 1994 and provided interchange initially at Custom House, between the DLR and the NLL.

EPS Feeder Services Begin

Feeder services from the East Coast main line, from Edinburgh Waverley to Waterloo International, were introduced by EPS on 3rd July 1995. These were intended to develop the market ready for the introduction of North of London Eurostar trains in 1996, which were dependent on the necessary infrastructure improvements taking place. The Up working left Edinburgh at 08.30 with the Down train leaving Waterloo Interna-

Class 59/0 No.59003 YEOMAN HIGHLANDER on a Merehead-Purfleet 'Yeoman' stone train, 14 May 1988. Photograph Brian Morrison.

tional for Edinburgh at 12.47. These trains utilised the North London incline from the East Coast main line to Camden Road and took the West London Line from Willesden Junction (High Level Junction), the same route as the one intended for Eurostar operation. These services were subsequently withdrawn.

Plans Reinstated

After re-evaluation of the modernisation project, on 27th July 1995 Railtrack announced plans to upgrade the NLL to 25kV overhead electrification, from Acton Central (earlier plans had started this work at South Acton) to Camden Road. This work would not only benefit Eurostar passengers, but would greatly reduce delays on NLRlys domestic services; these in turn had suffered from reliability problems caused mainly by ageing infrastructure – notably the electric equipment, signalling, tunnels and viaducts. Work commenced quickly and by mid-August 1995, Sunday possessions were in place to allow preparatory work to be undertaken.

NLR reintroduced its 'Towards Tomorrow' publicity campaign in September 1995, though there was less emphasis on engineering matters (now the responsibility of Railtrack) and much more on replacement service information and long term benefits to NLRlys customers. In October, a replacement timetable booklet 'Towards a new Tomorrow' was produced in a matter of days and widely distributed by teams of managers and staff at stations, through public libraries and other information outlets.

A seven month 'blockade' was required on the Willesden Junction-Camden Road via Hampstead Heath section, commencing Sunday 29th October. Without this central section the normal through services had to be separated into several sections and alternative arrangements sought with London Underground, London Buses and other bus operators for journeys not covered by the following replacement service:

Richmond - Willesden Junction (High Level) served by 2 trains per hour in each direction
Willesden Junction - North Woolwich served by 2 trains per hour in each direction
Camden Road - Stratford served by 2 trains per hour in each direction
Special Bus service (NL1) Willesden Junction station - Kilburn (Jubilee Line station) 4 buses per hour in each direction
Special Bus service (NL2) Camden Road - Gospel Oak 2 buses per hour in each direction

Buses were operated by Metroline and were painted in NLRlys blue/green house colours.

Station Improvements

Work on improving stations was included in the new scheme and major work was undertaken at:
Acton Central - reinstatement of the missing canopy on the Richmond bound platform
Brondesbury - new shelters
Brondesbury Park - new shelters
Camden Road - major refurbishment of the booking hall
Finchley Road & Frognal - rebuilt platforms and waiting accommodation
Hampstead Heath - demolition of the 1950s built platform buildings and cano-
pies, replaced with period style canopies and shelters
Gospel Oak - Major repairs and redecoration to enhance booking hall
Kensal Rise - Provision of ramp to westbound platform and refurbishment of entrance and booking hall
Kentish Town West - repainting of station

Underneath the Arches

The work was scheduled for completion on 1st June 1996 but had to be extended when Railtrack engineers removed rails and ballast from the trackbed of the Camden Road-Gospel Oak section, which runs entirely on brick built viaduct. The arches underneath were found to be in need of major structural repair and the decision was rightly taken to tackle the problem and delay reopening, rather than reopen the line and have to institute another lengthy blockade at some time in the future.

As a result. the Willesden Junction-Camden Road section did not reopen to through traffic until 29th September 1996, thus allowing the first through trains to run over the whole route from Richmond to North Woolwich for 28 months. Since May 1994, the section Stratford to North Woolwich had been closed to allow the Jubilee Line Extension work, and did not reopen until the day that the Acton Central-Camden Road work began.

The NLL had not benefited from such investment since ownership by the old North London Railway and was now better equipped to handle traffic then at any time in its history.

A diverted train, the 6.50am Kings Lynn-Liverpool Street, approaching Canonbury on 14 May 1988. Locomotive is Class 47/4 No.47581 GREAT EASTERN, in early style NSE livery. Photograph Brian Morrison.

Class 56 No.56053 coming off the North London Link Line from Acton Wells at Acton (the line continues on over the bridge in the background to South Acton) with down Yeoman hoppers, 13 July 1990. On the WR main line the Class 121 unit is on an up Greenford; the Brush Class 47 is on the down main. Photograph Colin J. Marsden.

Western Junction signalbox at Dalston; the derelict curve under Boleyn Road marks the former line to Broad Street. Class 313 set No.010 restarts the 11.35am North Woolwich-Richmond train from Dalston Kingsland on 30 April 1990. Photograph Brian Morrison.

313 set No.005 (forming the 17.35 North Woolwich-Richmond) approaching Acton Wells on 28 July 1992. Photograph Colin J. Marsden.

The 17.52 Liverpool Street-Watford awaits departure on the final day prior to withdrawal of the service at Liverpool Street on 25 September 1992. Flooding at Primrose Hill station meant the planned stop there had to be abandoned – hence the NOT appended to the already crude 'headboard'. Photograph Brian Morrison.

Chapter Seventeen
A Bright Future

Under New Ownership

The 1993 Railways Act brought about the privatisation of Railtrack in 1995 and after half a century ownership of the track and buildings passed once more into private hands. Passenger rolling stock had been vested in three train leasing companies and these too passed into private ownership from 1995. The Government offered twenty-five train operating companies of the British Railways Board as franchises lasting between five and fifteen years. The European Passenger Services Eurostar operation was included as part of the package, to attract a private sector promoter to build the Channel Tunnel Rail Link (CTRL).

The NLRlys franchise was one of the last to be offered by the Office of Passenger Rail Franchising (OPRAF) to prospective new owners. The process began in October 1996 and by December three companies had been shortlisted to 'work up' their proposals – Connex Rail, National Express Group and Great Western Holdings. On 24th January 1997 it was announced that National Express Group had been selected as the preferred bidder. National Express Group took over the NLRlys franchise on 2nd March 1997 with a 7½ year franchise. The company has traded as Silverlink since October 1997, and had announced several plans for improvements to the North London Line, including refurbishment of the

Class 313 units and a number of innovations for improving security on both trains and stations. As indicated in the franchise agreement, the old diesel multiple units used on the Gospel Oak-Barking line were replaced by modern Class 150 units during 1999. Silverlink trains now carry distinctive branding to complement the purple, green and yellow livery.

London & Continental Railways

As part of the privatisation process, the building of the proposed Channel Tunnel Rail Link from the Tunnel to St Pancras passed to London & Continental Railways (L&CR), which also took over responsibility for the terminus station at St. Pancras and operation of the former British Rail element of Eurostar. L&CR were taking forward the plans to operate Eurostar services north of London when the company announced it was unable to raise the necessary capital to build the Channel Tunnel Rail Link (CTRL) for which Parliamentary approval had been obtained. Faced with a difficult decision, Deputy Prime Minister John Prescott negotiated a rescue package which resulted in responsibility for funding of the first stage of the CTRL passing to Railtrack. This was the section from the Tunnel to Fawkham Junction, near Gravesend, a distance of 42 miles. Construction began at the end of 1998 and the line is due to

open in 2003. These plans were announced on 3rd June 1998. Railtrack also has an option to build the 26 mile section from Fawkham Junction to St Pancras via Stratford, for completion in 2007. The concession to build and operate the CTRL is for ninety years, until 2086, when ownership will revert to the Government.

As part of the same rescue package, a consortium comprising British Airways and National Express took over the operation of the Eurostar services in conjunction with Belgian (SNCB) and French (SNCF) national Railways. At the time of going to press, the new operators were evaluating the operation of Eurostar North of London services.

Virgin Rail, one of the partners in the original Eurostar agreement, also bid to take over the Eurostar services. Virgin had indicated a willingness to operate the North of London services if the new operators of Eurostar declined to do so.

LTS Rail Plans for West Ham

In May 1996 the franchise to operate London Tilbury & Southend services was awarded to Prism, which operates the franchise as LTS Rail. Prism's submission to the Franchising Director included the reinstatement of the LT&S platforms at West Ham station, thus making interchange with the LUL District, LUL

The old terminus building at North Woolwich was acquired by the Passmore Edwards Museum Trust and opened as a railway museum by Her Majesty Queen Elizabeth, the Queen Mother, in November 1984. The Queen Mother arrived behind LNER Pacific No.4472 FLYING SCOTSMAN.

Jubilee and NLL possible on completion of the necessary work. The new platforms opened in the late eighties. Services on this route are now branded c2c.

Connex introduce WLL line services

Connex South Central, part of the CGEA Group from France, introduced a new Rugby-Gatwick Airport service in June 1997. This service operates over the WLL between Willesden Junction and Clapham Junction and calls at Kensington Olympia. This has opened up a large number of journey opportunities and has seen passenger numbers grow considerably since introduction. Connex lost South Central franchise on 26 August 2001, and services on the route are now operated by Govia who will operate the service as Great Southern Railway.

The Docklands Light Railway Privatised

The Docklands Light Railway (DLR) was privatised on 6th April 1997 with Docklands Railway Management Ltd awarded a seven year franchise.

Future Plans

There have also been a number of plans announced for the future and these will ensure that the NLL continues to develop in a manner which would have made the original promoters proud. Not all will reach fruition, but in a capital city where public transport plays such a major role, it is important to put forward schemes with the potential to reduce congestion and create new journey opportunities.

A New Station for Richmond?

In December 1995 Railtrack announced plans for the rebuilding of Richmond station, providing the work could be funded in conjunction with a developer. No progress had been made at the time of going to press.

Willesden 'Hub'

In December 1995 the London Borough of Brent, in conjunction with its neighbouring local authorities Ealing and Hammersmith & Fulham, whose boundaries all meet at the station, secured a Single Regeneration Budget Bid (SRB) for funding the first stages of this scheme (see Chapter 16).

Preparatory work was funded early in 1996 by Harlesden City Challenge and involved removal of a former local authority nuclear bunker, installation of CCTV cameras to improve personal security, rebuilding the footpath from Harrow Road and reinstatement of the former Harrow Road booking office, to make a new entrance to the station. A new station entrance, along with major improvements to the station were unveiled on 27 October 2000 by Susan Kramer, Chair of Transport for London. The plans reinstating the slow line platforms on the main line have not been progressed.

West Hampstead

Over the years there have been numerous suggestions for a new station to cover all lines in the West Hampstead area

(The LUL's Jubilee and Metropolitan Lines and the Railtrack-owned Chiltern, Thameslink and North London Lines). From time to time, suggestions reappear on agendas of local authorities and transport organisations. In early 1999 proposals to take this further were released for consultation.

East London Line Extension

There is every likelihood that most of the abandoned section of the former Broad Street line from Dalston Western Junction to Shoreditch will be reopened in the next few years. This forms part of the plan for the northern extension of London Underground's East London Line. The East London Line currently runs from Shoreditch to Whitechapel and then on to New Cross and New Cross Gate, passing beneath the River Thames between Wapping and Rotherhithe. These proposals were the first to go before Parliament under the Transport & Works Act (1992).

The scheme was granted legal powers in January 1997. At the time of going to press it is planned for construction to commence in 2002, with an opening two years later. Stations are planned at Bishopsgate (replacing Shoreditch), Hoxton, Haggerston and Dalston Junction.

The Chelsea - Hackney Line

The initial consultation document for the proposed Chelsea to Hackney Line of London Underground Ltd (published March 1995), also included options for using the NLL east of Highbury & Islington. At the time of going to press, these plans have not progressed beyond the discussion stage.

The Woolwich River Crossing

Work continues on the planning of the Woolwich River Crossing, linking lines in north and east London with those to the south. Crossing the River Thames between Silvertown and Woolwich gives the NLL unlimited potential. These plans have not yet progressed beyond the planning stage.

Heathrow City Link

In October 1996 Richard Branson's Virgin Group announced plans for a rail-air link from the City to Heathrow Airport. From a terminus at Moorgate, it is proposed that trains would utilise Thameslink tracks from Moorgate to Cricklewood, where they would join the Cricklewood-Dudding Hill-Acton Wells line. At Acton Wells the link between Acton and Acton Main Line would give access to Ealing Broadway and the Heathrow Express link beyond Hayes & Harlington, to gain access into the new link opened in June 1998, from the Great Western main line to stations underneath the airport Terminals. Heathrow Express is owned by the British Airports Authority (BAA), owners of Heathrow and other airports.

In December 1996 BAA announced its own plans for a St. Pancras-Heathrow Airport service. This would operate via the Cricklewood-Acton Wells line and

join the Great Western main line using the Acton Wells-Acton link. Services would use Heathrow Express units with the line being modernised and electrified with 25kV overhead catenary. At the time of going to press, these plans are still being evaluated.

New WLL Stations

A number of station plans continue to be discussed under the leadership of Railtrack. An interchange with the LUL District Line at West Brompton was officially opened on 27th May 1999.

Gospel Oak - Barking Line Electrification?

With 25kV electrification already in place at both ends of this line and on the short central section through South Tottenham, full electrification has been put forward by Railtrack for future consideration. In the meantime, Silverlink Trains introduced Class 150 diesel multiple units to the line later in 1999. These became surplus from another National Express Group franchise – Central Trains – which ordered new units for some of its services. These replaced the ageing 1959/60 built Class 117 diesel units used on Gospel Oak-Barking line services in recent years.

Docklands Light Railway City Airport Extension

On 17th June 1998 Deputy Prime Minister John Prescott announced approval for a direct link from the DLR's Beckton line to serve London City Airport and the adjacent developments alongside the Royal Albert Dock. Again, no timescale has been given for this project.

Stratford International Station

When the second stage of the Channel Tunnel Rail Link is built to St. Pancras from Kent, it is planned to build an International station at Stratford. This will have a major impact on the NLL and the other lines that serve the current Stratford station. The DLR had published proposals for extending its services to this new facility, which is likely to be built on railway land in close proximity to the existing station. Stratford International is not scheduled for completion before the year 2007.

Conclusion

Never in railway history can a line have survived two major closure attempts and then been elevated from local to the brink of international passenger status! But this is not the end of the story, for as London's roads become more congested, the transport planners are once again looking to rail. The future of lines in North London is now in the hands of its owners, operators, politicians, planners, developers, neighbours and passengers. Great lessons can be learned from history. Now we have established where we have come from, those responsible for our railways will be able to plan where they are going in the years that lie ahead. I have every confidence that they will do so.

Appendix 1 - Stations served by North London Railway and its successors

Name	Notes	
Acton	Opened	1st August 1853
	Renamed	Acton Central from 1st January 1925
Bath Road Halt	Opened	8th April 1909
	Closed	1st January 1917
Blackwall	Opened	To North London Railway services 1st September, 1870*
		*opened by London & Blackwall Railway, 6 July 1840
	Closed	To North London Railway services 1st July, 1890*
		*closed by London & North Eastern Railway, 4th May 1926
Bow	Opened	26th September 1850
	Closed	15th May 1944*
		*last day of rail service – official closure date 23rd April 1945
Brentford Road	Opened	1st January 1869
		Renamed Gunnersbury from 1st November 1871
Broad Street	Opened	1st November 1865*
		*Official Civic Opening 31st October 1865
	Closed	27th June 1986
Brondesbury Park	Opened	1st June 1908
Caledonian Road	Opened	10th June 1852
	Renamed	Barnsbury from 1st July 1870
		Resited to east, 21st November 1870
	Renamed	Caledonian Road & Barnsbury from 22nd May 1893
Camden Town	Opened	7th December 1850
	Renamed	Camden Road from 1853
	Renamed	Camden Town from 1st July 1870
		Resited to west, 5th December 1870
	Renamed	Camden Road from 25th September 1950
Dalston Junction	Opened	1st November 1865
	Closed	27th June 1986
Edgeware [sic] Road (Kilburn)	Opened	2nd January 1860
	Renamed	Edgware Road & Brondesbury from 1st January 1872
	Renamed	Brondesbury (Edgeware Road) from 1st January 1873
		Renamed Brondesbury from 1st May 1883
Fenchurch Street	Opened	To North London Railway services 26th September 1850*
		*opened by London & Blackwall Railway, 2nd August 1841
	Closed	To North London Railway services 31st December 1868*
		*Station still open
Finchley Road (St. Johns Wood)	Opened	2nd January 1860
	Renamed	Finchley Road & Frognal from 1st October 1880
Hackney	Opened	26th September 1850
		Resited to west, 1st December 1870
	Closed	15th May 1944*
		*Last day of rail service. Official closure date 23rd April 1945
		Reopened as Hackney Central 12th May 1980
Hackney Wick	Opened	12th May 1980
Haggerston	Opened	2nd September 1867
	Closed	6th May 1940
Hammersmith	Opened	8th April 1858
	Renamed	Hammersmith & Chiswick from 1st July 1880
	Closed	1st January 1917
Hampstead Heath	Opened	2nd January 1860
Hampstead Road	Opened	9th June 1851
		Resited 5th May 1855
	Renamed	Chalk Farm from 1st December 1862
	Closed	1st January 1917
	Reopened	10th July 1922
	Renamed	Primrose Hill from 25th September 1950
	Closed	28th September 1992
Homerton	Opened	1st October 1868

	Closed	15th May 1944*
		*last day of rail service – official closure date 23rd April 1945
	Reopened	13th May 1985
Islington	Opened	26th September 1850
	Renamed	Islington & Highbury from 1st June 1864
	Renamed	Highbury & Islington from 1st July 1872
Kensal Green & Harlesden	Opened	1st November, 1861
		Resited 1st July 1873, opened as Kensal Green
	Renamed	Kensal Rise from 24th May 1890
Kentish Town	Opened	2nd January 1860
	Renamed	Gospel Oak from 1st February 1867
Kentish Town	Opened	1st April 1867
	Renamed	Kentish Town West from 2nd June 1924
	Closed	18th April 1971*
		*Date of last trains, official closure 20th December 1976
	Reopened	5th October 1981
Kew	Opened	1st August 1853
	Closed	to regular services, 1st February 1862
	Closed	to all passenger services, 1st October 1866
Kew (Bridge)	Opened	1st February 1862
	Renamed	Kew Bridge from December 1868
	Closed	12th September 1940 (LMS station, SR station adjacent still open)
Kew Gardens	Opened	1st January 1869
Kingsland	Opened	9th November 1850
	Closed	1st November 1865
	Reopened	As Dalston Kingsland, 16th May 1983 (completely new station)
Liverpool Street	Opened	To North London Line trains 30th June 1986*
		*Opened by Great Eastern Railway 2nd Feb 1874
	Closed	To North London Line trains 28th September 1992*
		*Station still open
Maiden Lane	Opened	1st July 1887
	Closed	1st January 1917
Mildmay Park	Opened	1st January 1880
		Closed 1st October 1934
Newington & Balls Pond	Opened	1st September 1858
	Renamed	Canonbury from 1st July 1870
		Resited to west 1st December 1870
Old Ford	Opened	1st July 1867
	Closed	15th May 1944*
		*Last day of rail service officially closed 23rd April 1945
Poplar East India Road	Opened	1st August 1866
	Closed	15th May 1944*
		*Booking office remained open for bus service until 23rd April 1945
Richmond	Opened	To North London services 1st January 1869*
		*opened to London & South Western services from 27th July 1846
Rugby Road Halt	Opened	8th April 1909
	Closed	1st January 1917
Shoreditch	Opened	1st November 1865
	Closed	4th October 1940*
		*Official closure date 17th November 1941
South Acton	Opened	1st January 1880
Victoria Park (Hackney Wick)	Opened	14th June 1856
	Renamed	Victoria Park from 1859
		Resited To south, 1st March 1866
	Closed	8th November 1943
West End Lane	Opened	1st March 1888
	Renamed	West Hampstead from 5th May 1975
Willesden Junction	Opened	1st September 1866
	Closed	Main Line platforms only, 3rd December 1962*
		*Remainder of station remains open
Woodstock Road	Opened	8th April 1909
	Closed	1st January 1917

The 12.25 service from Tottenham Hale to North Woolwich approaches its destination on 10 August 1973, formed of a three car BRCW DMU (later Class 110) made up of DMCL No. 50549 leading TBS No. 59253 and DMCL No. 50547. Brian Morrison.

Appendix 2 - Goods Depots served by North London Railway and its successors

Acton Coal
(located at Acton Gate House Junction)

	Opened	1867
	Closed	4th January 1965

Acton Goods

	Opened	1867 (to coal 1856)
	Closed	1st March 1965

Blackwall Goods & Coal (GNR)*
*Located on former London &
Blackwall Railway

	Opened	1900
	Closed	1961

Bow Coal

	Opened	1851
	Closed	c1874

Bow Goods
(L&NWR)

	Opened	20th March 1893 on site of Bow Coal
	Closed	1940

Broad Street
(L&NWR)

	Opened	18th May 1868
	Closed	27th January 1969

Caledonian Road Coal

	Opened	1851
	Resited	1869
	Transferred	To L & NWR 1st September 1871 and opened for general goods traffic
	Closed	6th September 1969

Camden Road (Lockett's Coal)

	Opened	December 1851
	Transferred	To L & NWR 1871
	Closed	1940

Devons Road Goods(L&NWR)

	Opened	July 1874 for coal, February 1891 for general goods
	Closed	2nd November 1964

Dunloe Street (L&NWR) -
See Shoreditch Finchley Road

	Opened	c1870
	Closed	2nd January 1967

East India Docks Goods (GER)

	Opened	June 1848
	Closed	6th March 1967

Graham Road (Hackney Downs) (GER)

	Opened	May 1894
	Closed	4th October 1965

Hackney Goods

	Opened	20th October 1850
	Transferred	To L&NWR, 1871
	Closed	4th October 1965
	Closed	4th October 1965

Hackney Wick Goods (GNR)

	Opened	1st March 1878
	Closed(tem)	June 1877
	Reopened	1st March 1878
	Closed	9th October 1967*
		*Some records show 6th November 1967

Hammersmith Coal & Goods

	Opened	1st May 1857
	Closed	3rd May 1965

Hampstead Heath (L&NWR)

	Opened	1st March 1863
	Closed	30th September 1972

Highbury

	Opened	as Islington, 20th October 1851
	Renamed	Highbury (coal) 1864
	Transferred to LNW and resited to north-west 22nd December 1872 for general goods
	Closed	4th August 1969

Kentish Town Goods (L & NWR)

	Opened	1862
	Closed	7th August 1972

Kew Goods

	Opened	July 1856 as a coal depot and for general goods from 1863
	Renamed	Kew Bridge North, 1948
	Closed	c1980

Kingsland (Coal, later Goods)
(NLR and L & NWR)

	Opened	for coal, 20th October 1851
	Extended	for general goods, 1st November 1870
	Closed	7th August 1972

Maiden Lane (Cattle, later Goods)
(later L & NWR)

	Opened	24th June 1867
	Transferred	to L & NWR for goods and cattle, 7th January 1868 – resited in 1870s on north side of line
	Closed	1965
	Reopened	As Freightliner depot, 15th November 1965
	Closed	As Freightliner depot, May 1968

Old Ford Goods

	Opened	1868
	Transferred	to L & NWR, 1st November 1870
	Closed	6th November 1967

Poplar Goods (GWR)

	Opened	1st April 1878
	Closed	October 1940 (Destroyed by bombing)

Poplar Goods (NLR)

	Opened	20th October 1851 for coal, 1st January 1852 for general goods
	Closed	c1980

Poplar Goods (L&NWR)

	Opened	12th March 1853
	Closed	c1980

Poplar Goods (GNR)

	Opened	1st September 1868
	Closed	c1980

Shoreditch (Dunloe Street Goods)

	Opened	March 1893*
		*Fully opened 4th April 1893
	Closed	3rd June 1968

South Acton Milk Depot

	Opened	not known
	Closed	not known

Worship Street Goods

	Opened	not known
	Closed	3rd March 1969